Corporate Acquisitions and Mergers in France

Charles-Henri De Pardieu
Patrick Jais
Sampiero Lanfranchi
Thierry Bellot

De Pardieu Brocas Maffei
Bellot Mullenbach & Associés

This book was originally published as a chapter in Corporate Acquisitions and Mergers.

General Editor: Peter Begg

Wolters Kluwer
Law & Business

Published by:
Kluwer Law International
PO Box 316
2400 AH Alphen aan den Rijn
The Netherlands
Website: www.kluwerlaw.com

Sold and distributed in North, Central and South America by:
Aspen Publishers, Inc.
7201 McKinney Circle
Frederick, MD 21704
United States of America
Email: customer.service@aspenpublishers.com

Sold and distributed in all other countries by:
Turpin Distribution Services Ltd.
Stratton Business Park
Pegasus Drive, Biggleswade
Bedfordshire SG18 8TQ
United Kingdom
Email: kluwerlaw@turpin-distribution.com

ISBN 978-90-411-5269-5

This title is available on www.kluwerlawonline.com

Corporate Acquisitions and Mergers in France

De Pardieu Brocas Maffei

De Pardieu Brocas Maffei is a Paris-based, independent French law firm recognized for its strong international practice. Established in 1993, the firm advises French and foreign clients, mainly industrial or commercial groups and banking establishments. It is active in the field of international financial and commercial transactions, mergers and acquisitions, banking and finance, real estate and real estate finance, litigation and arbitration.

Charles-Henri de Pardieu was admitted to the Paris Bar in 1965 and is the firm's senior and founding partner. A specialist in the field of international business law, he has extensive experience in banking and finance law, acquisitions and corporate restructurings, as well as real estate transactions.

Patrick Jais was admitted to the Paris Bar in 1987 and is a partner of De Pardieu Brocas Maffei. His practice focuses on corporate matters, including mergers, acquisitions, divestitures, joint ventures, and, more generally, all aspects of corporate law, stock exchange regulations, complex reorganization, and commercial litigation (including stock exchange and white collar litigations). He has significant experience advising French and foreign companies, including French and foreign listed companies, investment funds and industrial groups.

Sampiero Lanfranchi is an associate of Pardieu Brocas Maffei. His practice focuses on corporate and contractual matters, stock exchange regulations and litigations matters.

Bellot, Mullenbach & Associes BM&A

Thierry Bellot from 'Bellot Mullenbach & Associés', accounting and financial audit firm recognized as special expert with the Paris Court of Appeal (http://www.bma-paris.com/). Thierry Bellot, chartered accountant, auditor and expert to the Paris Court of Appeal, set up the firm in 1979, which became Bellot Mullenbach et Associés in 2003. With his firm, he works with all the BM&A service lines, with particular emphasis on activities relating to company transactions, measurement, independent appraisals and legal auditing for business transfers and mergers, and the financial recovery of companies under-performing or in financial distress. Thierry Bellot is an elected member of the Conseil Supérieur de l'Ordre des Experts-comptables (High Counsel of the French Association of Chartered Accountants), of which he chairs the Prevention Committee.

Address:
57 avenue d'Iéna
5116 Paris
France

Tel.: 33153577171
Fax: 33153577170
Website: www.de-pardieu.com

Contents

INTRODUCTION

[01] Alongside European harmonization of laws and standards, French law is going through an ongoing process of adaptation as the result of the constant evolution of international business and finance practice and to meet the expectation and needs of the development of French companies. France is also developing specific rules to reinforce its competitiveness as a financial market and its 'attractiveness' to foreign investors (see information on the website of the Invest in France Agency of the French government, <www.invest-in-France.org/fr>). The 2005 report of the World Bank set France as top reformer within the European countries for reduction in time and cost for business start up (*Doing Business in 2005: Removing obstacles to growth*). Furthermore, the 2010 report of the World Bank emphasizes that France significantly improved its regulation with regard to the insolvency process, reduced time needed to transfer properties, and made it easier to obtain encumbrance and ownership documents from the registry (*Doing Business in 2010: European Union*).

[02] The French practice of mergers and acquisitions does not differ from the international standards for private companies (due diligence, private bids, letter of intent, share purchase agreement, reps and warranties, etc.) or for listed companies. Transactions regarding listed companies must comply with French financial or market rules harmonized with European directives or issued by NYSE Euronext Paris, which operates the French stock markets. The key word for listed companies is 'transparency': i.e., France was one of the first European countries to reinforce its law after the Enron failure (Financial Security Act, *loi de sécurité financière No. 2003-706* promulgated on 1 August 2003).

[03] A specificity of the French law of mergers and acquisitions is the large choice of corporate structures; nevertheless, recent changes in law allow more and more flexibility (particularly with regard to drafting articles of association) and the differences between these corporate structures are becoming less clearly defined.

[04] The first part of this chapter presents a general overview of the corporate environment in France, while the second addresses the prior administrative and other consents which must be obtained in relation to French merger and acquisition transactions. Merger and acquisition techniques are then reviewed, and related tax considerations are covered. Finally, issues related to labour law in the context of mergers and acquisitions are addressed.

[05] Please note that some French words which have a specific meaning according to French law cannot be translated into English without leading the reader astray; this is why French words have been used below, following their translation in English.

NB French laws and regulations are codified; the different codes in force can be consulted on <www.legifrance.gouv.fr.> and for listed companies, the regulations of the ***Autorité des Marchés Financiers*** (AMF) is available in French and in English on <www.amf-france.org>.

CORPORATE OVERVIEW

Common Forms of Legal Entities in France

Branches versus Subsidiary Companies

[06] Foreign companies may conduct business in France either through branches or subsidiaries.

A *branch* is a mere office opened by the foreign company in France that has no legal independent personality. As a result, the foreign mother company is jointly and severally liable for the debts of its branch. Under French tax rules, a branch is a permanent establishment in France and is liable for the payment of the same amount of taxes as any other legal entity in France. Branches, as foreign entities having their head office abroad, may conduct business in France subject to prior registration with the Trade and Companies Registry *(Registre du Commerce et des Sociétés)*. The conversion of a branch into a subsidiary may result in a transfer of business, and therefore must comply with the rules governing such transfer, and may give rise to payment of transfer and/or capital gain taxes.

[07] Foreign companies interested in doing business in France also have the option of assessing the French market through sales representatives (employees of the foreign company in France), sale agents (via self-employed individual or sale agency agreements entered into by the sale agent with a French company in order to act on behalf of the foreign company), or by opening a liaison office in France, in order to minimize administrative charges and procedure. A liaison office is entitled to prospect the market and advertise for the foreign company's products, but it cannot conduct any business and shall consequently be treated as a branch as soon as it starts doing business.

[08] A *subsidiary* is a separate legal entity incorporated in France: the foreign parent company is not liable for the subsidiary's debts, and the losses of the subsidiary cannot be offset against the profit of the parent company, subject to rules described below for *sociétés civiles* and *sociétés de personnes*. A corporate entity is incorporated in France as of the date of its registration with the Trade and Companies Registry. Under French law, a company can be created by two or more individuals or legal entities, French or foreign, except when French company law provides for a legal form of companies which can be created by a single individual or legal entity

Sociétés Civiles versus *Sociétés Commerciales*

[09] Distinction between *sociétés civiles* and *sociétés commerciales*: Companies are organized for gain and profit, as opposed to *associations*, which bring together individuals or entities for non-profit making purposes. French company law makes a distinction between 'commercial companies' (or *sociétés commerciales*), which pursue business, trading or commercial objectives and 'non trading companies' (or *sociétés civiles*), whose purpose under French law is considered as non commercial (or *civil*), such as agriculture, real estate, mining, intellectual activity (writing, music, sales of artwork by artists, research), and professional activities (consulting, law, architecture, physicians, medicine, dentistry, etc.). It should be noted that 'non commercial purpose' does not necessarily exclude commercial concerns.

[10] *Sociétés civiles* are regulated by Articles 1832 to 1873 of the French Civil Code, Decree No. 78-704 and 78-705 of 3 July 1978. *Sociétés commerciales* are regulated by Articles 1832 to 1844-17 of the French Civil Code, Articles L.210-1 to L.252-12 and Articles R.210-1 and seq. of the French Commercial Code, Decree No. 78-704 of 3 July 1978. These provisions set out a statutory framework applicable to the various types of companies which can be registered in France.

[11] In addition to the legal forms of company referred to herein above, there are other forms of special entities under French law, such as the *groupement d'intérêt économique* ('GIE') or in English 'economic interest group', which is a special legal entity created for the purpose of facilitating or developing the economic activity of its members, and whose activities must be ancillary to those of its members. There is also the *société en participation* (silent and unincorporated partnership), which is a collective enterprise whose partners have decided not to register and which is therefore not a separate legal entity, distinct from its partners.

Sociétés Civiles

[12] Main features of a *Société Civile*: a *société civile* is an entity formed between at least two partners who may be individuals or legal entities. The French Civil Code does not set forth a minimum amount of share capital but each partner must contribute to the company either in cash (*apport en numéraire*) or in kind (*apport en nature*). The interests in the capital are represented by shares called *parts sociales* issued by the *société civile* to remunerate the contributions of the partners. A partner may also contribute his/her expertise or knowledge, services or work (*apport en industrie*); such contribution is not taken into account in the share capital, however shares may still be allocated to such contributors. The share capital need not be paid up immediately after the issue of the shares or by a specific deadline.

[13] Profits and losses of the company are allocated to the partners in accordance with the articles of association, which may provide that such allocation is different from the allocation of shares between the partners. However, allocating all the profits or all the losses to one or several partners, or depriving one partner of any portion of the profits, or exempting one partner from any losses is prohibited under French law. Each partner is liable for the *société civile*'s debts in proportion to his/her/its ownership interest at the date the liability arises (or at the date the *société civile* is declared bankrupt). The partner who contributed his/her expertise or knowledge, services or work (*apport en industrie*) is considered to have the same share in the capital as the lowest partner in equity.

[14] A partner remains liable for the liabilities until the date of the transfer of his/her/its shares has been notified to the company and filed with the clerk of the Commercial court.

[15] Transfer of shares of a *Société Civile*: The *parts sociales* (shares) are considered as partners' claims against the company and therefore are transferable as claims by a deed of transfer (executed in as many original copies as parties, except for the case of a deed of transfer drafted by a *notaire* (or 'notary public' in English) who is a public officer in France, plus an original copy to be filed with the tax authorities and two with the clerk of the Commercial court in the jurisdiction in which the *société civile* is registered. The Notice of transfer must either be given to the company by service of process or acknowledged in an official deed.. Any transfer of shares (including by donation or contribution in kind and transfer between partners) are subject to the prior approval of the partners (or the general manager). Furthermore, the articles of association can require a prior approval for transfer by merger or split-up, or transfer to parents and descents of partners or conversely the articles of association can exempt from prior approval any transfer of shares between partners or to a partner's spouse. If the transfer is not approved, the partners must purchase the shares or cause the shares to be purchased within six months (unless otherwise provided in the articles of association).

[16] Shares of a *société civile* can be pledged; such pledges are recorded by the clerk of the Commercial court.

[17] Management and partners' decisions: A *société civile* is run by one or several general managers called *gérants*. The partners can appoint as *gérant* individuals or legal entities, partner or non-partner, French or alien.

[18] The *gérant* is vested with all necessary powers to act and to represent the company and no limitation placed on the powers of the *gérant* is binding *vis-à-vis* bona fide third parties. The *gérant* appointed by the partners may delegate part of his powers to an employee of the *société civile*.

[19] The *gérant* is liable to the *société civile* and third parties for violations of the law, breaches of the articles of association and misconduct in the management of the company. The *gérant* can be dismissed by a decision of the majority of the partners unless otherwise stipulated in the articles of association. Dismissal of a *gérant* without real cause shall give right to damages.

[20] Except for *sociétés civiles* carrying out a regulated activity for which the law may provide specific rules such as majority and quorum rules for partners' decisions, the articles of association govern the decision-making process of the *société civile*: majority rules for ordinary decisions or extraordinary decisions (it be noted that extraordinary decisions usually are those which amend the articles of association), and if no majority rule is fixed by the articles of association, the partners decisions are taken unanimously. The articles of association can provide for written consultation of the partners. Collective decisions may also result from consent expressed by all the partners in a private written agreement (*acte sous-seing privé* or *acte ssp*) or official deed (*acte authentique*) drafted by a notary public. Partners meetings are convened by registered letters with a fifteen-day prior notice period. A breach of the convening rules may not be raised later to oppose decisions if all the partners attend or are represented at the meeting.

[21] Partners must meet or take a decision once a year for the approval of the annual accounts within six months following the end of each financial year.

[22] The main advantages of the structure are its flexible organization and the limited corporate formalities during the lifetime of the company. There are also tax advantages which may determine the choice of this structure as a result of its fiscal transparency; however the *société civile* can decide to opt for the same fiscal regime as commercial companies (see below). *Sociétés civiles* are the legal form of corporate most currently used to hold real estates.

Sociétés commerciales

[23] ***Sociétés de personnes* versus *sociétés de capitaux***: There are two main types of commercial companies: (i) the *sociétés de personnes* (private companies) and (ii) the *sociétés de capitaux* (joint stock companies).

[24] *Sociétés de personnes* (private companies) bear high similarities with *sociétés civiles* in terms of organization and operating process, including the transfer of *parts sociales*: the identity of partners joining the company is a critical factor (*intuitu personae*), and the partners' liability for the corporate debts is unlimited. However contrary to *sociétés civiles*, partners of *sociétés de personnes* are considered as *commerçants* (merchants), and consequently, their liability for corporate debts is joint and several (except limited partners in *société en commandite simple*). There are two types of *sociétés de personnes*: the *société en nom collectif* ('SNC') and the *société en commandite simple* ('SCS'). *Sociétés de personnes* are prohibited from going public.

[25] ***Sociétés de capitaux*** (joint stock companies): The *intuitu personae* of the shareholders of *sociétés de capitaux* is not an essential factor. The underlying principles of this corporate form are the limitation of liability of the shareholders to their respective contributions to the share capital and the free transfer ability of the shares (unless specifically provided otherwise). A *société de capitaux* is commercial whatever its corporate object. However, by contrast with the SNC or SCS, its shareholders do not acquire the status of 'merchant' (except general partners of *société en commandite par actions* who are merchants). The shareholders' liability is limited to their respective contributions to the share capital. The three types of *sociétés de capitaux* are (1) the *société anonyme* ('SA', French equivalent to a corporation), (2) the *société en commandite par actions* ('SCA') and (3) the *société par actions simplifiée* ('SAS'). These companies are also called *sociétés par actions*, which means that their capital is divided by shares (*actions*). To favour the development of the capital markets, French company law sets out a statutory framework applicable to *sociétés de capitaux* with respect to the provision of information to the shareholders and the exercise of shareholders' rights. Thus shareholders have little latitude to organize their relationships within such companies, with the exception of *société par actions simplifiée* ('SAS') which as described below is the only *sociétés par actions* which cannot go public.

[26] Another kind of company, the *société à responsabilité limitée* ('SARL', French equivalent to a limited liability company) has the same characteristics of each of *sociétés de personnes* and *sociétés de capitaux*: the identity of the partners joining the company is a critical factor (*intuitu personae*), its capital is divided into *parts sociales*, but the partners' liability is limited to their contribution and they are not merchants. The *SARL* is prohibited from going public.

[27] It should be noted that the distinction made under French company law between *sociétés de capitaux* and *sociétés de personnes* is mitigated in practice for a number of reasons: the importance of the identity of the partners in the *sociétés de personnes* may be diminished by stipulating in the company's articles of association that, for example, the death of a partner will not result in the dissolution of the company, which may survive with the partner's heirs. Conversely, in the *sociétés de capitaux*, the identity of the shareholders may be reinforced by the insertion of a prior approval clause (*clause d'agrément*) regarding transferees of the shares in a close company.

[28] Medium or small-sized companies are essentially incorporated for tax and social security reasons, although an individual can very often, from an economic viewpoint, run his or her business individually without incorporating a legal entity. For this reason, the *société à responsabilité limitée* (SARL), which offers simplicity of organization combined with limited liability, is the most common corporate structure in France.

[29] Due to the flexibility of its organization, the *société par actions simplifiée* (SAS) is becoming the most common form of incorporation in France, except for large publicly held companies and businesses requiring substantial capital investment, for which the *société anonyme* (SA) remains the form required to go public. Pursuant to European Council Regulation No. 2157/2001 of 8 October 2001 on the Statute for a European company and Articles L.229-1 and *seq.* of the French Commercial Code, a *societas europaea* (SE) with its head office in France should be organized as a *société anonyme.*

[30] According to French statistics agency (INSEE), 549 788 new *sociétés commerciales* were registered in 2011 (622 000 in 2010, 152 300 in 2009), among which 79% were SARL. The statistics emphasize 88% of 549,788 companies registered during 2010 where individual companies (*entreprises individuelles*) and 94% were self-employed *(auto-entrepreneurs).* According to the statistics of the clerk of the Commercial court of Paris for 2011, 50% of the *sociétés commerciales* registered in *Paris were SARL, 19% were SA or SAS, 1,5% were SNC or GIE, and 26% were sociétés* civiles..

[31] French *sociétés par actions* as SA, SCA or SAS may issue different categories of shares and securities, including preferred shares (*actions de préférence*), negotiable bonds, warrants (*bons de souscription*). Securities issued by French *sociétés par actions* are dematerialized and are recorded in the issuing company's books.

Main Characteristics of the Different French *Sociétés Commerciales*

[32] The main characteristics of the most common corporate forms of French commercial companies are briefly set out below.

Sociétés de personnes

Société en Nom Collectif (SNC)

[33] An SNC, or 'General Partnership' in English, is a company formed between at least two partners who may be individuals or legal entities, French or foreign. Each partner is considered as merchant (*commerçant*) and is accordingly indefinitely and jointly and severally liable for the corporate debts.

[34] There is no minimum share capital requirement and the share capital need not be paid up immediately after the issue of the shares or by a specific deadline. The interests in the capital are represented by shares which are not freely transferable: a transfer of shares to other partners or to third parties remains subject to the unanimous consent of the other partners notwithstanding any provision to the contrary in the articles of association.

[35] The sharing of profits and losses is determined by the articles of association of the SNC. It is possible to allocate to one partner a proportion of the results which does not necessarily correspond to his or her share in the capital.

[36] The sharing of profits may be different from the sharing of losses. However, it is unlawful to allocate to one or several partners all the profits or all the losses, to deprive one partner of any portion of the profits or to exempt one partner from any losses.

[37] The decision-making process is flexible, by comparison with other corporate forms: a partners' meeting must be held in the following three cases: (i) for the approval of the annual accounts, (ii) when a meeting is convened at the request of a partner, and (iii) for the approval of a change in share capital in the context of a proposed safeguard or judicial reorganization plan. Unless otherwise provided for in the articles of association, all other decisions may be taken by written consultation or consent expressed by all the partners in a private written agreement (*acte sous-seing privé*) or a notarial deed drafted by a notary public (*acte authentique*). Pursuant to the French Commercial Code, the following decisions require the unanimous consent of the partners: a sale of interest-share in the SNC, the dismissal of a managing-partner when all the partners are managers or when the managing-partner being dismissed was nominated in the articles of association, the continuation of the partnership after the dismissal of a partner-manager, the continuation of the partnership despite the bankruptcy, the incapacity or the legal obstacle to the continued participation of one of its partners (such partner will not take part to the vote), the conversion of the legal form of the company into a *société par actions simplifiée* ('SAS' or 'simplified stock company') or the takeover of the company by an SAS.

For all of the other partners' decisions, majority decision-making is permitted if provided for in the articles of association.

[38] All the partners are in principle equally responsible for the company's management, including its day-to-day management. The articles of association may provide that the SNC may have one or several *gérants* (i.e., managers) who may be French or foreign, individuals or legal entities, chosen among the partners either by unanimous consent (when nominated in the articles of association) or according to the majority rules set forth in the articles of association. A *gérant* is vested with all necessary powers to act for and to represent the company and no limitation placed on the powers of a *gérant* shall be binding *vis-à-vis* bona fide third parties. A *gérant* appointed by the partners may delegate a portion of his or her powers to employees of the SNC.

[39] When all the partners are *gérant* or when the *gérant* is a partner nominated in the articles of association, the dismissal of the *gérant* requires the unanimous consent of the other partners and usually causes the winding up of the company, provided that the articles of association do not state otherwise or the partners do not decide otherwise. When the *gérant* is a partner not nominated in the articles of association, his/her dismissal must be decided as provided in the articles of association or by unanimous consent of all the other partners. When the *gérant* is not a partner, he can be dismissed by a decision of the majority of the partners, unless provided otherwise in the articles of association.

[40] Similar to shares of *sociétés de personnes,* the shares of the SNC are not negotiable instruments and can only be transferred by a written deed of transfer (executed in as many original copies as parties, except for the case of a deed of transfer drafted by a notary public, plus an original copy to be filed with the tax authorities and two with the clerk of the Commercial court in the jurisdiction in which the SNC is registered). Notice of the transfer must be given to the company either by service of process, by acknowledgment in an official deed or by acknowledgment by the *gérant* upon receipt of an original of the deed of transfer at the registered office.

[41] All transfers of shares (including between partners) are subject to the prior approval of all of the partners. Except as otherwise provided for in the articles of association, the company automatically dissolves when a partner dies.

[42] The SNC shares can be pledged; such pledges must be recorded by the clerk of the Commercial court in the jurisdiction in which the company is registered.

[43] The main advantages of the SNC structure are its flexible organization and the limited corporate formalities during the lifetime of the company. However, since the individual relationship between the partners is essential in an SNC, this type of company implies a close cooperation between a limited number of partners. There are also tax advantages which may determine the choice of this structure, especially as a result of the fiscal transparency of an SNC (see below).

[44] The joint and several liability of the partners for all corporate debts, and the extension of bankruptcy to all the partners when the SNC declares bankrupt are the essential disadvantages of the SNC corporate form. However, the issue of a partner's unlimited liability is solved in case a partner is a legal entity with limited liability. Furthermore, when a partner refuses to authorize the sale of interest-share in the SNC, no transfer of shares can take place, and there is no legal obligation for the partners to purchase such shares or cause the shares to be purchased.

[45] The appointment of a statutory auditor is mandatory when at the close of a fiscal year two of the three following thresholds are reached: the total of the balance sheet (assets or liabilities) is over EUR1,550,000, the turnover (excluding VAT) is over EUR3,100,000 or the average number of employees is over fifty.

Société en Commandite Simple (SCS)

[46] The main feature of the *société en commandite simple* or 'limited partnership' in English, is the existence of two categories of partners:

- one or several general partners called *commandités*, who manage the company and are indefinitely and jointly and severally liable for the corporate debts, as are the partners of an SNC (the rules of the French Commercial Code for the partners of the SNC are applicable to the general partners of the SCS);
- one or more limited partners called *commanditaires* who contribute to the share capital and whose liability is limited to their contribution in the share capital, provided they do not actively take part in the management of the company (contrary to the SNC partners, they are not merchants).

[47] As in an SNC, there is no minimum set by law on the amount of share capital; and the share capital does not need to be fully paid up.

[48] The SCS is managed by a *gérant* who may be selected from among the commandités or from among third parties. In theory, a *commanditaire* cannot become a *gérant* without losing his status of *commanditaire*, since he/she would then become indefinitely and jointly and severally liable for the corporate debts. The rules previously set out for the appointment, dismissal and scope of authority of the *gérant* in an SNC apply equally to the *gérant* in an SCS.

[49] A partners' meeting must be held in the following three cases: (i) for the approval of the annual accounts; (ii) when a meeting is convened at the request of a general partner or 25% of the limited partners, and (iii) for the approval of a modification of the share capital during a safeguard procedure or a judicial restructuring. The partners' decision-making process is the same as in the SNC. The unanimous consent of the general partners and the consent of the majority of the limited partners are required for any amendments to the articles of association. However, the unanimous consent of all the partners (general and limited) is required for the change of the company's nationality, the conversion of the legal form of the company into a *société par actions simplifiée* or an SNC and the takeover of the company by a *société par actions simplifiée*.

[50] Shares cannot be transferred, including between partners, without the unanimous consent of the partners. However, the articles of association can provide that (i) the shares of the limited partners can be freely transferred among the partners, and that (ii) the shares of the general or limited partners can be transferred to a third party subject to a prior consent of all the general partners and of the majority limited partners. Transfers of shares take place in the same manner as transfer of shares of an SNC.

[51] The same rules as for the SNC apply for the designation of a statutory auditor when the same thresholds are reached.

[52] The SCS is rarely used in practice, given that it has the same disadvantages as the SNC, especially with respect to the *commandités* (joint and several liability) without offering the same flexibility (the structure is complex with the *commandités* and *commanditaires* having different legal status) and without offering the same tax advantages, since the SCS, unlike the SNC, does not have complete fiscal transparency.

Société à Responsabilité Limitée (SARL)

[53] An SARL is regarded as commercial regardless of its corporate purpose. However, its shareholders do not acquire the status of merchant. Shareholders' liability is limited to their respective contributions to the share capital.

[54] An SARL may have only one shareholder (in such a case the SARL is called an *entreprise unipersonnelle à responsabilité limitée* or EURL) but cannot have more than hundred shareholders. The shareholders may be French or foreign individuals or legal entities (please note that an EURL cannot be the sole shareholder of another EURL).

[55] There is no minimum share capital required by law; however the articles of association must fix an amount for the share capital (which can be a variable amount of capital) divided into shares (*parts sociales*). Shares representing a contribution in kind must be totally paid up at the time they are issued; shares representing a contribution in cash may be partly paid up (subject to a minimum of 20% of the par value of each share) at the time they are issued, the remaining amount being paid up over the next five years as and when called by the *gérant*. A shareholder can contribute his/her expertise, knowledge, services or work ('apport en industrie'); such contribution is not taken into account in the equity capital but shares may be allocated to such contributor. Any subscription premium should be entirely paid up upon subscription. The SARL may not go public. The articles of association must indicate the allocation of the shares among the shareholders. Since 2004, Article L.223-11 of the French Commercial Code authorizes the issuance of registered bonds (*obligations nominatives*) by an SARL under specific conditions.

[56] Similar to shares of *sociétés de personnes,* the shares of the SARL are not negotiable instruments and can only be transferred by a written deed of transfer (executed in as many original copies as parties, except for the case of a deed of transfer drafted by a public notary, plus an original copy to be filed with the tax authorities and two with the clerk of the Commercial court in the jurisdiction in which the SARL is registered). Notice of the transfer must be given to the company either by service of process, by acknowledgment in an official deed or by acknowledgment by the *gérant* upon receipt of an original of the deed of transfer at the registered office.

[57] The transfer of shares to third parties is subject to the prior approval of the majority of the shareholders representing at least half of the shares, unless if the

articles of association provide for a higher majority. Please note that except as otherwise provided in the articles of association, the shares may be freely transferred between shareholders and to a shareholder's spouse, ascendants or descendants.

[58] The extraordinary shareholders' meeting has a three-month period of time from the notification of the planned transfer to consent to or refuse the transfer of shares; if it has not made its decision known within this period of three months, the consent to the transfer shall be deemed obtained. If the shareholders' meeting refuses to consent to the transfer, the shareholders are held, within a period of three months as from the notification of such refusal made by registered letter return receipt requested to acquire or to have acquired the shares at a price agreed between the parties or, in the absence of agreement between the parties, at a price determined by an expert appointed either by the parties or by the president of the Commercial court pursuant to Article 1843-4 of the French Civil Code, unless the transferor waives his or her plan to transfer shares. At the request of the *gérant* this period of time can be extended by court decision without such extension exceeding six months. The company may also, with the consent of the transferring shareholder, resolve within the same period of time to reduce its capital by the amount of the par value of the shares and to repurchase the shares at a price determined as provided above. A period of payment which may not exceed two years may, on justification, be granted to the company by court decision. The amounts due shall bear interest at the legal rates usual in commercial matters. If on expiration of the allotted time limit none of the solutions set forth above have taken place, the transferring shareholder may complete the transfer initially contemplated.

[59] Furthermore, since the 2 August 2005 Act (No. 2005-882) relating to small and medium enterprises, shares of an SARL may be rented out to individuals if permitted by the articles of association.

[60] The shares of an SARL can be pledged; such pledges are recorded by the clerk of the Commercial court within the jurisdiction in which the company is registered. If the company has consented to a plan to pledge company shares under the same conditions as for the approval of shares' transfer, such consent shall automatically constitute approval of the transferee in the case of forced sale of shares in accordance with the provisions of Articles 2346 and 2347 of the French Civil Code, unless the company chooses to immediately repurchase the shares to reduce share capital following the transfer.

[61] An SARL is managed by one or more *gérants* (general manager) who must be individuals but who need not be shareholders. The *gérants* are appointed either by the articles of association or by an ordinary shareholders' meeting deciding by a majority of more than 50% of the existing shares unless the articles of association provide for a higher majority. Their term of office may be a specific duration or for an unlimited period.

[62] An SARL *gérant* may be dismissed by the ordinary general shareholders' meeting by a majority of more than 50% of the existing shares, unless the articles of association provide for a higher majority. A dismissal may give rise to damages if not supported by equitable cause (*juste motif*).

[63] *Gérants* are vested with the broadest powers to act on behalf of the company in all matters *vis-à-vis* third parties, in all circumstances, subject to the powers expressly attributed by law to the shareholders. The company is bound even by those acts of *gérant(s)* unrelated to the company's purpose, unless it establishes that the third party knew that such an act exceeded such purpose. In its relations with the shareholders, in the absence of any provision to the contrary, the *gérant(s)* may conduct all acts of management in the interest of the company.

In the event of there being several *gérants*, each shall hold separately the powers described above. The opposition which one *gérant* may make to the acts of another *gérant* shall be without effect as regards third parties, unless it is established that they have knowledge of such opposition. The *gérant*(s) may grant, under their responsibility, any special or temporary delegations of power for determined transactions to any authorized representative of their choice.

[64] The company is liable for the acts of the *gérant* except when these acts are outside the corporate purpose and when the company can prove that third parties knew that such acts were outside the scope of the corporate purpose. The *gérant* is liable for acts which violate the statutory rules and regulations governing SARLs and the company's articles of association or for serious mistakes committed while managing the company. A shareholder may sue the *gérant* for his or her own damages or on behalf of the company, for damages suffered by the company.

[65] The company cannot lend money or grant any guarantee to its *gérants* or its shareholders who are individuals. According to Article L.223-19 of the French Commercial Code, the *gérant(s)* or if applicable, the statutory auditor must submit to the shareholders' meeting a report on any transactions concluded directly or indirectly between the company and its *gérant(s)* or shareholders. These formalities do not apply to regular transactions concluded under arm's length conditions. The shareholders' meeting must approve this report. The interested *gérant(s)* or shareholder cannot participate in the vote and his or her shares shall not be included in the calculation of the quorum and majority. However, if there is no statutory auditor, transactions concluded by a *gérant* who is not a shareholder are subject to the prior approval of the shareholders' meeting. Transactions that have not been approved are nevertheless binding, the interested *gérant*, and if applicable the interested shareholder being jointly and severally liable for adverse consequences of the transaction for the company. These provisions of Article L.223-19 of the French Commercial Code also apply to transactions concluded with a company of which a severally responsible shareholder, *gérant*, director, *Directeur Général*, member of the *Directoire* or member of the Supervisory Board, is simultaneously a *gérant* and a shareholder of the company.

[66] Shareholders decisions are taken in general shareholders' meeting; however, the articles of association may provide that these decisions may be taken, at the option of management, at a general meeting, through consultation by mail, or by an instrument expressing the consent of all shareholders. A shareholders meeting is required to approve the financial statements for each fiscal year. Furthermore one or several shareholders representing either one quarter of the shareholders and one quarter of the shares or representing one half of the shares can request a shareholders' meeting. Since the Modernization of the Economy Act (Law n°2008-776 of 4 August 2008), articles of association of SARL can provide for shareholders meetings by teleconference or videoconference.

[67] Meetings are called by the *gérant* by registered letter fifteen days in advance. All shareholders are entitled to attend general meetings. Each shareholder has the right to participate in collective decisions and has a number of votes which corresponds to his or her shares. Each shareholder may be represented by another shareholder (provided that the total number of shareholders exceeds two) or by his or her spouse. The articles of association may provide that a shareholder may be represented by a non-shareholder.

[68] Those decisions by the shareholders which do not relate to the amendment of the articles of association are considered to be ordinary. Each year, within six months following to the end of the fiscal year, the shareholders must be convened by the *gérant(s)* in order to approve the accounts of that fiscal year and to allocate the profits. In order to be valid, ordinary decisions must be adopted by one or more shareholders representing at least half of the share capital. If such majority is not obtained, decisions are made, on second vote, by a majority of votes cast, regardless of the proportion of capital represented. However, decisions relating to the appointment or removal of a *gérant* shall only be valid if taken by one or more shareholders representing at least half of the share capital.

[69] An extraordinary shareholders' meeting is required by French company law whenever the articles of association are amended. Extraordinary decisions are validly passed: (1) unanimously, for decisions to change the company's nationality, increase one shareholder's liability, convert the company to a *société en nom collectif; société en commandite simple, société par actions simplifiée*, for the decision of a takeover of the company by a *société par actions simplifiée*; (2) by a majority of the number of shareholders representing at least half of the company's shares, for decisions to admit a new shareholder or authorize the pledge of shares; and (3) in accordance with the 2 August 2005 Act (No. 2005-882) relating to small- and medium-sized enterprises, if the company was incorporated before 4 August 2005, all other extraordinary decisions are validly passed by the shareholders representing at least three quarters of the shares, but if the company was incorporated after 4 August 2005, to be validly passed all other extraordinary decisions require a quorum of one quarter of the shares (one fifth on a second call) and a majority of two thirds of the attending or represented shares (or a higher majority which cannot be unanimity).

[70] Each share gives its owner a right to the corporate assets and profits to an extent proportional to the number of shares held, unless otherwise provided by the articles of association. However, as well as for other corporate forms, it is unlawful to allocate all the profits to one or several shareholders or to exempt a shareholder from any losses.

[71] French Commercial Code provides for a template of articles of association to form a single person limited liability company (EURL) by an individual who is concurrently the sole shareholder and the general manager. The use of this template is optional.

[72] The appointment of a statutory auditor is mandatory when at the close of a fiscal year two of the three following thresholds are reached: the total of the balance sheet (assets or liabilities) is over EUR1,550,000, the turnover (excluding VAT) is over EUR3,100,000 or the average number of employees is over fifty.

[73] For medium-sized companies, the choice between limited liability companies should be essentially made between the SA, the SAS and the SARL. For small-sized companies, this choice should be essentially made between the SAS and the SARL. The simplicity of the SARL over the SA is an advantage. The absence of a minimum share capital of the SARL when a minimum of EUR37,000 is required for the SA is also an advantage. The mandatory regulatory frame of the SARL is an asset as the company can be formed or operated without a lawyer's assistance. However, since 1 January 2009, the SAS offers some advantages similar to those of the SARL, as no minimum share capital is required and the appointment of a statutory auditor becomes mandatory only when the same thresholds are reached. The flexibility of the SAS may be an advantage to organize a company but that corporate form usually requires more skills and professionalism, particularly when it comes to drafting the articles or association.

Sociétés de capitaux

Société Anonyme (SA)

[74] An SA requires a minimum of seven shareholders (there is no maximum). The shareholders may be French or foreign individuals or legal entities.

[75] The minimum share capital for a privately held SA is EUR37,000 divided into shares (*actions*). The change of the legal definition of a company going public by an *ordonnance* dated 22 January 2009 suppressed the minimum requirement of EUR225,000 for a company going public. The minimum par value per share may be established by the articles of association. The indication of the par value in the articles of association is not mandatory.

[76] The contributions to the share capital made by shareholders may be contributions in cash and/or in kind. A shareholder cannot contribute his/her expertise or knowledge, services or work (*apport en industrie*).

[77] Shares representing a contribution in kind must be totally paid up at the time they are issued. Shares representing a contribution in cash may be partly paid up (subject to a minimum of 50% of the par value of each share at the formation of the company and of 25% of the par value of each share in case of increase of the share capital) at the time they are issued, the remaining amount being paid up over the next five years as and when called by the Board of Directors. Any subscription premium should be entirely paid up upon subscription.

[78] Management of the SA: Board of Directors or *Directoire* and Supervisory Board. An SA can be managed either by a Board of Directors (*Conseil d'administration*), or by a management board or directorate (*Directoire*) under the control of a Supervisory Board (*Conseil de Surveillance*).

[79] The SA with a Board of Directors (traditional model): Since 2001 (Law on new economic regulations of 15 May 2001, or the 'NRE Law'), the operational or day-to-day management of an SA with a Board of Directors is assumed by an individual whether or not a director, appointed by the Board, to hold the title of *Directeur Général* (chief executive officer). The Chairman of the Board of Directors (*Président du conseil d'administration*), elected by the directors from among themselves may be appointed as *Directeur Général*, with the consequent title of *Président Directeur Général* ('PDG').

[80] The Board of Directors is composed of a minimum of three and a maximum of eighteen members (since 1 January 2009, except otherwise provided for in the articles of association, the directors are not required to be shareholders). Directors may be either French or foreign individuals or legal entities. When a legal entity is appointed as director, it must designate a representative (*représentant permanent*) who incurs the same liability as if he or she were appointed as director. When the articles of association required to appoint the directors from among the shareholders, the newly appointed director who is not a shareholder of the company at the time of his or her appointment, must become a shareholder within six months (three months before 1 January 2009) failing which he or she shall be deemed to have resigned by operation of law. The directors are appointed (or dismissed) at the shareholders' meeting by the majority of the shareholders present or represented (ordinary general shareholders' meetings). In the event of a vacancy due to the death or resignation of one or more directors, the Board of Directors may, between two shareholders' meetings, provisionally fill the vacancy. The appointment of the directors by the Board of Directors is submitted for ratification at the next ordinary shareholders' meeting. Any director so appointed to replace another director shall remain in office only for the remainder of his or her predecessor's term of office. According to the law of 23 March 2012, the articles of association set the term of office of the directors, which cannot exceed six years. The same law provides the possibility for a director to be employee of a SA if (i) the company does not exceed the thresholds set out in Article 2 of EU recommendation 2003/361/CE (a company which employs fewer than 250 persons, has an annual turnover not exceeding EUR50 million and/or an annual balance sheet total not exceeding EUR43 million), (ii) if employment contract corresponds to effective employment.

Any appointment for a period of more than six years should be void.

[81] Except as otherwise provided in the articles of association, the number of directors over the age of 70 years may not be more than one third of the directors in office.

[82] An employee of the company can only become a director if his or her contract of employment relates to real work for the company. The number of directors bound to a company by a contract of employment may not exceed one third of the directors.

[83] The office of director cannot be remunerated (including by allocation of stock options). However the annual shareholders' meeting may allocate to the Board a lump sum to be shared among its members to compensate them for their attendance at the Board meetings, called *jetons de présence* or attendance fees. A director may receive a special compensation for a special and extraordinary task.

[84] The Board of Directors must appoint from among its members a Chairman, who must be an individual, and a *Directeur Général*, who must be an individual but who is not required to be a director nor a shareholder. The Chairman of the Board of Directors organizes and oversees its work and reports to the general shareholders meeting thereon. He or she ensures the smooth functioning of the company's management structures and, in particular that the directors are able to accomplish their task. Except as otherwise provided in the articles of association, the Chairman of the board cannot be over sixty-five years old. The board can decide to award the Chairman remuneration for his services. When it appoints the Chairman, the Board must choose whether to separate the offices of *Directeur Général* and Chairman of the Board or to combine these two offices in the same individual.

[85] The *Directeur Général* (or the PDG) assumes, under his or her responsibility, the general management of the company. He shall be vested with the most extensive powers to act on behalf of the company in all circumstances, subject to powers reserved to the shareholders' meeting or to the Board of Directors. He shall represent the company in its dealing with third parties. The *Directeur Général* may be assisted by one to five deputy chief executive officer(s) (*Directeur(s) Général(aux) Délégué(s)*), appointed by the board on the *Directeur Général*'s recommendation. The *Président du Conseil d'administration*, the *Directeur Général* and if any, the *Directeur(s) Général(aux) Délégué(s)* can be dismissed by a majority of the board, while board members can only be dismissed by a shareholders' meeting.

[86] The Chairman, the *Directeur Général* and the *Directeur(s) Général(aux) Délégué(s)* may be dismissed at any time by the Board of directors. The *Directeur Général* and the *Directeur(s) Général(aux) Délégué(s)* are entitled to damages in case of dismissal without equitable cause (*juste motif*), whereas the Chairman is not entitled to any form of compensation when dismissed from his or her functions, unless the dismissal is particularly injurious or unless he or she have an employment contract.

[87] The Board of Directors determines the strategic orientation and the broad lines of the company's business activities and ensures their implementation. Subject to the powers expressly invested in the shareholders' meetings, and in so far as the articles of association permit, it deals with all matters relating to the conduct of the company's business and decides all pertinent issues through its deliberations.

[88] In its dealings with third parties, the company is bound by acts of its Board of Directors even if they do not fall within the company's corporate purpose, unless it can prove that the third party knew that this specific action was outside to that purpose or, given the circumstances, could not have been ignorant of that fact. Mere publication of articles of association does not suffice to constitute such proof.

[89] The Board of Directors carries out any verification which it considers appropriate. The Chairman of the Board and the *Directeur Général* are required to provide each director with all the documents and information necessary to perform his or her mission.

[90] Guarantees and liens granted by an SA (other than banks or other financial institutions) must be authorized by the Board of Directors.

[91] The Board of Directors holds meetings in accordance with the provisions of the articles of association; however, on one hand, if the board has not met for a period of more than two months, the directors representing at least one third of the members of the board may take the initiative to convene a meeting and indicate the agenda, and, on the other hand, the *Directeur Général* may always request the Chairman to call a board meeting on a specific agenda.

[92] For any meeting to be valid, the personal attendance of at least half of the directors is required. Internal regulations of the Board of Directors may provide for directors who attend board meetings via videoconferencing or a telecommunication medium which permits their identification and guarantees their effective participation to be deemed to be present for calculation of the quorum and the majority, except for those decisions for which these means of participation are not permitted by law or the articles of association.

[93] Unless the articles of association require a higher majority, decisions are taken by a majority of the members present or represented. In case of a split vote, the Chairman of the meeting has a casting vote (except where otherwise provided by the articles of association).

[94] According to Article L.225-38 of the French Commercial Code, any agreements entered into, either directly or indirectly, between the company and its *Directeur Général*, one of its *Directeur(s) Général(aux) Délégué(s)*, one of its directors, one of its shareholders holding a proportion of the voting rights greater than 10% or, in the case of a corporate shareholder, the company which controls it, must be subject to the prior consent of the Board of Directors upon request of the interested party to the Chairman of the Board. These formalities do not apply to regular transactions concluded under arm's length conditions, but the Board of Directors and the statutory auditor must be provided with a list of these transactions. Agreements entered into between the company and another firm are also subject to prior consent if the company's *Directeur Général*, one of its *Directeur(s) Général(aux) Délégué(s)*, or one of its directors is the owner, a partner with unlimited liability, a *gérant*, a director or a member of that firm's supervisory board or, more generally, is in any way involved in its management. Please note that since 1 May 2005, any undertaking to pay compensation to a member of the board of a listed company by the company itself or an affiliate within the same group of companies (including any indemnities or allowances for dismissal) must also be submitted to the authorization process set forth by Article L.225-38 of the French Commercial Code.

[95] Once the Board has given its consent to the transactions, the statutory auditor must present to the shareholders' meeting a report on these transactions. The shareholders' meeting must approve this report. The interested shareholder(s) cannot participate in the vote and his or her shares are not included in the calculation of the quorum and majority. Transactions that have not been approved by the shareholders meeting are nevertheless binding on the company. However, the interested shareholder or board members are jointly and severally liable for adverse consequences of the transaction for the company. Transactions entered into without the prior authorization of the Board of Directors may be cancelled if they have prejudicial consequences for the company within three years from the date of the agreement. Nullity may be covered by a vote of the general meeting taken on the special report of the auditors setting out the circumstances by virtue of which the authorization procedure has not been followed.

[96] The company cannot lend money or grant any guarantee to its board members who are individuals, or to the *Directeur Général* or to the *Directeur(s) Général(aux) Délégué(s)*.

[97] In the double-tier form of the SA, the company is managed by a board of managers (the *Directoire* or directorate) under the continuous supervision of the Supervisory Board (the *Conseil de Surveillance*).

[98] The *Directoire* has a maximum of five members (seven if the company is listed) appointed by the Supervisory Board by a majority of the members present or represented for a time period of four years or for the time period set by the articles of association between two and six years. If the company's share capital is lower than EUR150,000, the *Directoire* may consist of a single member. The *Directoire* is formed of individuals, shareholders or not, French or foreign (members who are not citizens of EEC countries or OECD countries must obtain a merchant business card from the French authorities). Furthermore, members of the *Directoire* cannot be members of the Supervisory Board. Except as otherwise provided in the articles of association, the *Directoire*'s members cannot be over sixty-five years old. The Supervisory Board may decide to award remuneration to the *Directoire*'s members.

[99] Appointed by the Supervisory Board, the members of the *Directoire* are removed from office by vote of the general shareholders' meeting or, if allowed by the articles of association by a decision of the Supervisory Board. A dismissal without equitable cause (*juste motif*) may give rise to damages.

[100] The *Directoire* is vested with power to perform any act in the name of the company and any limitations on this power set out in the articles of association are unenforceable against third parties without notice. The Supervisory Board must appoint one of the *Directoire*'s members as President of the *Directoire*, to represent the company. The articles of association may provide that the company can also be represented by another member of the *Directoire* appointed by the Supervisory Board and named the *Directeur Général*.

[101] As French company law does not provide for the internal organization of the *Directoire*, the articles of association may determine (unlike in the traditional form of SA) when the *Directoire* must meet, the conditions in which a proxy may be given and the quorum and majority required to pass resolutions. Furthermore, it should be noted that there are no legal requirements as to the number of meetings.

[102] The Supervisory Board is composed of a minimum of three and a maximum of eighteen members (since 1 January 2009, except otherwise provided for in the articles of association, the Supervisory Board members are not required to be shareholders). Board members may be either French or foreign individuals or legal entities. When a legal entity is appointed as board member, it must designate a representative (*représentant permanent*) who incurs the same liability as if he or she were appointed board members. When the articles of association require to appoint the Board members from among the shareholders, the newly appointed member who is not a shareholder of the company at the time of his or her appointment, must become a shareholder within six months (three months before 1 January 2009), failing which he or she shall be deemed to have resigned by operation of law. The members are appointed (or dismissed) at the shareholders' meeting by the majority of the shareholders present or represented (ordinary shareholders' meetings). In the event of a vacancy due to the death or resignation of one or more members of the Supervisory Board, the Supervisory Board may, between two shareholders' meetings, provisionally fill the vacancy. The appointments of the members by the Supervisory Board shall be submitted for ratification at the next ordinary shareholders' meeting. Any board member so appointed to replace another board member shall remain in office only for the remainder of his predecessor's term of office. The articles of association set the term of office of the board members, which cannot exceed six years (three years for the first board members when the company is formed).

[103] Except as otherwise provided in the articles of association, the number of Supervisory Board members over the age of seventy years may not be more than one third of the board members in office.

[104] An employee of the company may only become a board member if his contract of employment relates to actual employment. The number of board members who are employees of the company may not exceed one third of the board members. The office of board member cannot be remunerated (including by allocation of stock options); however, the annual shareholders' meeting may allocate to the Board a lump sum to be shared among its members to compensate them for their attendance at Board meetings, called *jetons de présence* or attendance fees. A board member may receive special compensation for special and extraordinary task.

[105] The Supervisory Board must appoint from among its members a Chairman and a vice-chairman, who must be individuals but they are not required to be a board member nor a shareholder. The Chairman and the vice-chairman of the Supervisory Board are in charge of calling and chairing the Supervisory Board's meetings. The board may decide to award them remuneration.

[106] The Supervisory Board permanently supervises the *Directoire*'s management of the company. The assignment of real property, and the total or partial assignment of equity holdings require the Supervisory Board's approval. Any guarantees or liens granted by the company (other than banks or other financial institutions) must be authorized by the Supervisory Board. The *Directoire* presents a report to the Supervisory Board at least once each quarter. The Supervisory Board carries out all verifications which it considers appropriate.

[107] For any meeting to be valid, the personal attendance of at least half of the board members is required. Internal regulations of the Supervisory Board may, in the event of board members attending meetings via videoconferencing or other telecommunication medium, set forth rules which permit their identification and guarantees their effective participation to be deemed to be present for calculation of the quorum and the majority, except for those decisions for which these means of participation are not permitted by law or the articles of association.

[108] Unless the articles of association require a higher majority, decisions are taken by a majority of the members present or represented. In case of a split vote the chairman of the meeting shall have a casting vote (except if otherwise provided by the articles of association).

[109] According to Article L.225-86 of the French Commercial Code, any agreements entered into, either directly or indirectly, between the company and one of the members of the *Directoire* or the Supervisory Board, one of its shareholders holding a proportion of the voting rights greater than 10% or, in the case of a corporate shareholder, the company which controls it, are subject to the prior consent of the Supervisory Board upon request of the interested party to the Chairman of the Board. These formalities do not apply to regular transactions concluded under arm's length conditions, but the Supervisory Board and the statutory auditor must be provided with a list of these transactions. Agreements entered into between the company and another firm are also subject to prior consent if one of the company's *Directoire* or Supervisory Board members is the owner, a partner with unlimited liability, a *gérant*, a board member or a member of that firm's supervisory board or, more generally, is in any way involved in its management. Please note that since May 1, 2005 any undertaking to pay compensation to a member of the *Directoire* of a listed company by the company itself or an affiliate within the same group of companies (including any indemnities or allowances for dismissal) is also to be submitted to the authorization process set forth by Article L.225-86 of the French Commercial Code.

[110] Once the Supervisory Board has given its consent to the transactions, the statutory auditor must present to the shareholders' meeting a report on these transactions. The shareholders' meeting must approve this report. The interested shareholder(s) cannot participate in the vote and his or her shares are not included in the calculation of the quorum and majority. Transactions that have not been approved by the shareholders meeting are nevertheless binding on the company. However, the interested shareholder and board members are jointly and severally liable for adverse consequences of the transaction for the company. Transactions entered into without the prior authorization of the Supervisory Board may be cancelled if they have prejudicial consequences for the company within three years from the date of the agreement. Nullity is covered by a vote of the general meeting taken on the special report of the auditors setting out the circumstances by virtue of which the authorization procedure has not been followed.

[111] The company cannot lend money or grant any guarantee to the members of the *Directoire* or the Supervisory Board who are individuals.

[112] This double-tier form of SA separates management from ownership in a way which enables independent professionals to manage the company. These professional managers can enter into employment contracts with the company and thereby obtain greater job security. If removed by the shareholders without appropriate justification (*juste motif*), these managers can obtain damages.

[113] An individual cannot concurrently be appointed (i) to more than five Boards of Directors or Supervisory Boards of *sociétés anonymes* having their registered office in France, (ii) to more than one office as *Directeur Général* or *Directoire* member, or (iii) to more than five offices when taking into accounts any type of office in *sociétés anonymes* (the offices of Directeur Général and member of the Board of Directors in the same company count for one office). These restrictions are subject to special provisions of the law for companies within the same group of companies or for unlisted companies.

[114] General Shareholders' Meetings: The supreme authority in an SA lies with the general shareholders' meeting. The shareholders must be consulted on any decision which exceeds the scope of authority of the directors.

[115] Any shareholder is entitled to attend general meetings if he or she has paid up his shares to the extent required by the Board of Directors. Since 2001 (NRE Law of 15 May 2001), the articles of association cannot require that a shareholder own a minimum number of shares in order to attend ordinary general shareholders' meetings.

[116] Each shareholder has the same number of voting rights as the shares he or she owns or represents, although shares without voting rights may exist as described below and some companies' articles of association may restrict the voting rights allocated to each shareholder.

[117] Any resolution which does not require an extraordinary shareholders' meeting under French company law (i.e., resolutions that do not amend the articles of association or change the nationality of the company) may be passed by the ordinary shareholders' meeting.

[118] Resolutions of the ordinary shareholders' meeting are passed by a majority of the votes held by the shareholders present or represented, if these shareholders hold at least one fifth of all shares entitled to voting rights. If this quorum is not met, a second meeting must be called with no quorum requirement.

[119] Resolutions of the extraordinary shareholders' meeting are passed by a majority of two thirds of the votes held by the shareholders present or represented, if these shareholders hold at least a quarter of all shares entitled to voting rights. If this quorum is not met, a second meeting must be called with a quorum requirement of at least one fifth of all shares entitled to voting rights. Except for listed companies, the articles of association may provide for a higher quorum in shareholders' meetings. For purposes of the 'quorum' or the 'majority' requirements, the shareholders present (attending the meeting) or represented by proxy or voting by mail are considered as *present or represented*; the articles of association may provide for shareholders who take part in the meeting via videoconferencing or a telecommunication medium which permits their identification and guarantees their effective participation to be deemed to be present for calculation of the quorum and the majority.

[120] A proxy can only be granted to another shareholder (or the shareholder's spouse). A proxy sent by a shareholder to the company without mentioning a proxy holder (an 'in blank proxy') is valid and considered as voting in favour of the resolutions proposed or approved by the Board of Directors and against any other resolutions.

[121] A shareholder holding 50% or more of the voting rights can control the appointment of the management and the approval of the annual accounts, both of which are passed by a majority vote of the shareholders. However, absolute control of an SA requires the ability to pass extraordinary resolutions by a majority of two thirds of the voting rights present or represented. Extraordinary resolutions are required to amend the articles of association, which includes increase of capital and issuance of shares.

[122] Certain decisions cannot be taken by a simple decision of the extraordinary meeting because unanimous consent of all shareholders is required when one shareholder's liability is increased, such as the decision to transform the company into another corporate form resulting in unlimited liability for shareholders (such as *société en nom collectif*, *société civile*, *société en commandite simple* or *société en commandite par actions*), to increase the share capital by increase of the par value of the shares (except in the event of share capital increase by incorporation of reserves) or to change the nationality of the company.

[123] All shares and securities issued by French companies are dematerialized. The shares of an unlisted SA must be registered shares (*actions nominatives*) whereas shares of a listed SA may be either in bearer form (*actions au porteur*) or in registered form.

[124] Registered shares can either be placed into accounts maintained by the issuing company (*titres nominatifs purs*) or they are put into accounts held by an agent called a *teneur de compte-conservateur* (a bank or duly qualified broker) appointed by the issuer of the shares (*titres nominatifs administrés*). Shares registered in bearer form must be placed into accounts held by a *teneur de compte-conservateur*. Shares of listed companies can also be in an identifiable bearer form (*titres au porteur identifiables* or TPI) which enables the issuing company to know the holder of each share subject to a specific process.

[125] An SA may issue different kind of securities and have different classes of shares. In addition to ordinary shares, an SA may issue shares (*actions*) or bonds (*obligations*) with attached options (*bons*), or options convertible or exchangeable into shares, or other complex securities (*valeurs mobilières composées*).

[126] An SA may also create preferred shares (*actions de préférence*). The preferred share generally gives financial advantages over an ordinary share, such as:

- a larger share in profits;
- a preferred dividend;
- a larger part in any liquidation premium.

[127] Preferred shares may also be deprived of voting rights only if the issuing company has realized distributable profits during the two financial years preceding the creation of such shares. Preferred shares without voting rights cannot represent more than half of the share capital (one quarter of the share capital in listed companies) and cannot be owned by the directors of the company. These preferred shares without any voting rights give a right to a minimum preferred dividend, the amount of which is fixed by the law.

[128] An SA may also give double voting rights to all the registered shares which are fully paid up and recorded under the name of the same shareholder for a minimum of two successive years. Some companies also grant an increased dividend (not in excess of 10%) to any shareholder who has kept his or her registered shares fully paid up for a minimum two-year period. In listed companies, the number of shares giving right to an increased dividend cannot exceed for the same shareholder 0.5% of the share capital of the company. It should be pointed out that the granting of an increased dividend in the course of the life of a company is not possible if there are already existing bonds with attached options (*obligations avec bons*), convertible or exchangeable bonds or a complex stock giving right to shares.

[129] In addition to the right to vote, each ordinary share gives a right to the corporate assets and profits to an extent equal to the number of shares held, unless otherwise provided by the articles of association. It is nevertheless unlawful to allocate to one or several shareholders all the profits of the company or to deprive a shareholder of any share in the profits.

[130] Sharing in the losses does not need to be proportional to the shares held provided a shareholder's liability cannot exceed his or her contribution to the share capital and provided a shareholder cannot be exempt from any sharing in a company's losses.

[131] Unlike a *société de personnes*, the underlying principle in an SA, as in all *sociétés par actions*, is the free transfer ability of the shares. However, the articles of association may provide for some limitation on the transfer of shares, bearing in mind that no shareholder should be prevented from withdrawing from the company if and when he or she decides to do so. The following limitations are often included in the company's articles of association: prior approval by the Board of Directors of the company before any share transfer takes place (*clause d'agrément*), though this provision cannot apply to transfers of shares between spouses, parents and descendants; pre-emptive rights (*droits de préemption*); a prohibition against selling any shares during a certain period of time justified by the company's interests (*clause d'interdiction temporaire de cession*); an obligation on the part of a shareholder to sell all his or her shares to the company in the case of specific events defined in the articles of association (*clause de rachat forcé*). However, the French financial market authority, *Autorité des Marchés Financiers* (AMF) (see below), requires that such clauses be deleted from the company's articles of association if the company is listed on the stock exchange.

[132] An SA must appoint at least one statutory auditor and a deputy statutory auditor. Two statutory auditors are required in any SA whose accounts are consolidated.

[133] Although the administration of an SA is cumbersome and inflexible (in particular for shareholders' meetings), the SA is the appropriate form for a business whose capital requirements cannot be met by a limited number of shareholders or which needs to go public to finance its development. Until the 12 July 1999 Act (No. 99-587) which facilitated the formation of *société par actions simplifiée*, the SA was the most common French legal form for medium-sized or large companies in France.

[134] The traditional form of SA with a Board of Directors remains the most widespread form in France.

Société par Actions Simplifiée (SAS).

[135] Because French limited liability companies did not offer much flexibility compared with companies from other jurisdictions in terms of internal corporate organization, especially in the context of joint ventures, a simplified limited liability company structure was introduced into French company law in 1994 under the name of *société par actions simplifiee* or *SAS* (simplified joint stock company). The main distinguishing characteristic of this corporate form is the flexibility given to shareholders to adapt the articles of association to their specific objectives and to establish the framework of their internal organization. However, unless otherwise specifically provided by law for the SAS, the provisions of the French Commercial Code applicable to the SA also apply to the SAS.

[136] Until the 12 July 1999 Act (No. 99-587), a *société par actions simplifiée* could only be formed between two or more large companies. Since 1999, the SAS may have one or several shareholders and its shareholders may be individuals or legal entities, French or foreign.

[137] The Modernization of the Economy Act of 4 August 2008 modified rules governing the SAS, which becomes closer to the SARL than to the SA. Since 1 January 2009, there is no minimum share capital required by law (until 31 December 2008, a minimum of EUR37,000 was required as for the SA); however the articles of association must fix an amount for the share capital (which can be a variable amount of capital) divided into shares (*actions*). As provided for SARL, no statutory auditor is required when the company does not exceed thresholds set by decree and same simplified rules govern the approval of the annual financial statements for SAS and SARL with one single individual concurrently shareholder and general manager. Furthermore, since 1 January 2009, the SAS can issue non-assignable shares to remunerate contribution of expertise or knowledge, services or work (*apport en industrie*), such contribution was prohibited until the Modernization of the Economy Act for *société par actions*.

[138] The SAS can issue all kind of securities that the SA can, including preferred shares and bonds, but the SAS must be exclusively privately held and is prohibited from going public. The *ordonnance* dated 22 January 2009 (coming in force on 1

April 2009) pertaining to the change of the legal definition of a company going public, without reverting the prohibition of public offerings for SAS, authorizes (i) private placement techniques with qualified investors (by virtue of their legal status and/or financial capacity) or with a restricted circle of investors or when the denomination of the securities offered by the SAS amount to at least EUR50,000 per unit and (ii) the admission to trading on a regulated market of financial securities other than shares (such as debt instruments, financial contracts).

[139] The SAS is characterized by the flexibility conferred upon the shareholders with respect to the organization of the company's management and the shareholders' meetings. The only requirement set forth in the law governing the SAS is that an SAS must have a President (who does not have to be a shareholder). The office of the President can be filled by either an individual or a legal entity. The President is generally (but not necessarily) the sole representative of the SAS *vis-à-vis* third parties and, in such capacity, is vested with the broadest powers to act on behalf of the SAS. The articles of association may provide that the company may be represented by a *Directeur Général* or a *Directeur Général délégué*.

[140] The articles of association may also provide for a collective management body in addition to the office of the President (and of *Directeur Général* or *Directeur Général délégué*). The President may be assisted by a management committee (*comité de direction*) or a Board of Directors or may be controlled by a Supervisory Board. The terms and conditions regarding the functioning of the management, the powers of the President and of any other management body which may be created, their decision-making methods, and the manner in which management meetings may be held are defined in the articles of association.

[141] The legal restrictions relating to the holding of several offices in an SA do not apply to the management of an SAS. In other words, the President and any other legal representative of an SAS may hold several offices which are not included in the maximum number of offices one person can hold.

[142] Furthermore, the information which must be provided to shareholders and be filed with the clerk of the Commercial court for each fiscal year of an SAS is less comprehensive than the information which must be provided to shareholders of an SA; for example, the annual report of the Board of Directors of an SA must include a list of all offices and functions including pursuant to an employment agreement held by the officers of the company, whereas this obligation does not apply to an SAS.

[143] The conditions governing shareholders' meetings and the conditions under which resolutions are passed (quorum, majority rules, etc.) are defined in the articles of association. Shareholders can adopt resolutions during actual meetings, by mail, by teleconference, by videoconference, or in the form of written decisions. The types of decisions which must be adopted by the management (President, management committee, General Manager, Supervisory Board, etc.) or by the shareholders are defined in the articles of association. However, the following decisions may only be adopted by the shareholders: modifications of the capital, merger or split up of the SAS, transformation of the SAS into another type of corporate entity, dissolution of the SAS, appointment of statutory auditors and approval of the annual accounts and distributions of dividends.

[144] French labour law entitles workers council delegates to attend and participate in meetings of the management body to be designated in the SAS' by-laws (i.e., the President or the collective management body). The articles of association specify in respect of which organ the workers council is entitled to exercise its rights.

[145] Two representatives of the workers council can attend the shareholders meetings of SA companies. The same possibility is offered to workers councils of SAS companies.

[146] Prior approval clauses for the transfer of shares, even between shareholders, and withdrawal or exclusion clauses are permitted.

Société en Commandite par Actions (SCA)

[147] Similar to the *société en commandite simple* (SCS), the *société en commandite par actions* or *SCA* (partnership limited by shares) is characterized by its two different categories of partners: general partners (*associés commandités*) and limited partners (*actionnaires commanditaires*) who incur different levels of liability. General partners (*associés commandités*) manage the company, hold shares which are not negotiable (*parts sociales*) and are jointly and severally liable for the debts of the SCA for an unlimited amount, similar to the partners of an SNC or of an SCS (an SCA may have one or several *commandités*). Limited partners (*actionnaires commanditaires*) have the same status as the shareholders of an SA, they contribute to the share capital and receive in exchange shares which are negotiable (*actions*), and their liability is limited to their capital contribution. However, unlike shareholders of an SA, they cannot take part in the management of the company as *commanditaires*, although the same person may be a *commandité* and a *commanditaire*. The number of limited partners may not be less than three.

[148] To the extent they are consistent with the special provisions of the law for SCAs, the rules provided for *société en commandite simple* (SCS) apply to the *commandités* and the rules provided for *société anonyme* (SA) apply to the *commanditaires* of the SCA.

[149] Consequently, the SCA is similar to the SA. There is a minimum of three shareholders, or *commanditaires* and one *commandité*, in an SCA. Unlike the SCS, the SCA is not prohibited from going public. However, a listed company incorporated as an SA which decides to be transformed into an SCA must initiate a squeeze out process (*offre public de retrait*) and may withdraw from the stock exchange. The minimum share capital for a SCA is EUR37,000 divided into shares (*actions*). The change of the legal definition of a company going public by an *ordonnance* dated 22 January 2009 suppressed the minimum requirement of EUR225,000 for an SCA going public.. The rules concerning the share capital and the issue of shares and bonds are the same as for an SA, except that the SCA can have a variable share capital if provided for in the articles of association.

[150] The *commanditaires* are in the same position as the shareholders of an SA with regard to their liability, which is limited to the amount of their contribution, and their shares are freely negotiable and transferable under the same terms and conditions as those for the transfer of shares in an SA. Resolutions are passed by the *commanditaires* by the same majority as resolutions passed by the shareholders of an SA.

[151] The *commandités* are in the same legal position as the partners of an SNC. If not appointed as *gérants* of the SCA, they may nevertheless have access twice a year to the company's accounts and submit questions in writing regarding the management. Furthermore, they are entitled to receive a portion of the benefits as determined by the articles of association.

[152] The management of the SCA is carried out by one or several *gérant(s)* appointed from among the *commandités* or among third parties with the unanimous consent of the *commandités* and a 50% majority of the *commanditaires*, unless otherwise provided in the articles of association. The conditions of dismissal of the *gérant* are determined by the articles of association. The articles of association often provide that the decision of the *commandités* to dismiss the *gérant* should be taken with unanimous consent. Except as otherwise provided in the articles of association, the *gérant* cannot be over sixty-five years old.

[153] The SCA has a Supervisory Board composed of at least three members who shall be *commanditaires* and shall not be *commandités*.

[154] The Supervisory Board's mission is to assume the permanent supervision of the management of the company. It does not play a management role but merely controls corporate decisions together with the company's statutory auditors and submits an annual report with its recommendations to the annual general meeting of shareholders. To perform its mission, the Supervisory Board has the same powers as the statutory auditor. It may call a general meeting. Members of the Supervisory Board may be held legally liable for torts committed by a *gérant* which are not disclosed to the general meeting.

[155] The members of the Supervisory Board are appointed by the ordinary general shareholders' meeting. As opposed to the shareholders' meeting appointing the *gérant*, the *commandités* are not allowed to participate in the vote appointing the members of the Supervisory Board.

[156] The term of office of the Supervisory Board members is fixed by the articles of association. Unless the articles of association provide otherwise, the members of the Supervisory Board may be dismissed at any time by the ordinary general meeting of shareholders without cause (as is the case for directors of an SA). Conversely, the members of the Supervisory Board may resign without justification. Unless otherwise provided in the articles of association, the number of directors over the age of seventy years may not be more than one third of the directors in office.

[157] The SCA form enables a separation between capital and management, which remains independent, and offers flexibility in terms of corporate organization. An established management trying to secure sources of funding while maintaining its independence (such as in a leveraged buy-out) may thus have an interest in opting for the SCA form. This structure where the *commandités* and the *gérants* are quasi-irrevocable, is also appropriate if the company wishes to protect itself from hostile takeover bids. However, the decision to transform an existing SA into an SCA should be carefully considered, especially if the SA is already listed, as this results in the delisting of the company.

European Company (SE)

Council Regulation (EC) of 8 October 2001 (No. 2157/2001) on the Statute for a European Company (known by the Latin term 'Societas Europaea' or SE) and Council Directive 2001/86/EC of 8 October 2001 supplementing the Statute for a European company with regard to the involvement of employees were implemented in France by the 26 July 2005 Act on Reliability and Modernization of the Economy (No. 2005-842), decree No. 2006-448 of 14 April 2006 on corporate aspects and decree No. 2006-1360 of 9 November 2006 448 with regard to the involvement of employees. The SE's registered in France are governed by Articles L.229-1 to L.229-15 of the French Commercial Code, Regulation (EC) No. 2157/2001 and the provisions of the French Commercial Code relating to *sociétés anonymes* when they are not in contradiction with Regulation (EC) No. 2157/2001. An SE can be the sole shareholder of another SE, in which case the provisions governing the *entreprise unipersonnelle à responsabilité limitée* (EURL) are also applicable. Since 2006, a very small number of SE have been incorporated in France, either holding companies or subsidiaries of foreign group.

[158] Regulation (EC) No. 2157/2001 provides four ways of forming an SE: merger, formation of a holding company, formation of a joint subsidiary, or conversion of a public limited company previously formed under national law. Formation by merger is available only to public limited companies from different Member States. Formation of an SE holding company is available to public and private limited companies with their registered offices in different Member States or having subsidiaries or branches in Member States other than that of their registered office. Formation of a joint subsidiary is available under the same circumstances to any legal entities governed by public or private law. A public limited company can convert into a SE if it has a least one subsidiary in a Member State other than that of its registered office.

[159] The SE must have a minimum capital of EUR120,000. French SE having specified activities (banking, insurances, investment services) must have a higher minimum capital, according to Regulation (EC) 2157/2011.

[160] The registered office of the SE designated in the articles of association must be the place where it has its central administration, that is to say its true centre of operations. The extraordinary shareholders' meeting may decide to transfer the registered office to another Member State. The shareholders who oppose this transfer can request the purchase of their shares. The company's debtors may oppose the transfer of the registered office subject to an earlier payment or the granting of guarantees. Since law on measures to adapt French corporate Law with European Law of 3 July 2008 (n°2008-649), the general attorney (*Procureur de la*

République) can oppose such a merger or a transfer of registered office abroad on behalf of the French State or upon request of any person or authority when such a transaction is contrary to public interest.

[161] The SE is registered in France with the trade and companies register held by the clerk of the Commercial court in the jurisdiction in which its registered office is located. Furthermore, according to EC regulations, the registration and completion of the liquidation of an SE must be disclosed for information purposes in the *Official Journal of the European Communities*.

[162] The articles of association of the SE must provide as governing bodies the general meeting of shareholders and either a management board (*Directoire*) and a Supervisory Board (two-tier system) or a Board of Directors (single-tier system) according to the provisions set by French law for the *société anonyme*. However, there is no mandatory quorum of at least half of the board members for the Board of Directors' meetings and for the Supervisory Board's meetings. Furthermore the Supervisory Board may appoint one of its members to exercise the functions of member of the *Directoire* in the event of temporary vacancy. During such a period the function of the person concerned as a member of the Supervisory Board is suspended.

[163] When the SE is not public, the articles of association may provide (i) any restriction to the free negotiability of the shares, subject to a ten-year time limit, (ii) that a shareholder can be obliged to sell his or her shares in specific circumstances, or (iii) that a shareholder must inform the SE of any change of control in its shareholding and that the SE may decide to suspend its non financial rights (voting rights) in the SE or to squeeze it out. Such provisions, which are valid in an SAS, are questionable in an SA in view of the 'negotiability' of the shares.

[164] To comply with the Council Directive 2001/86/EC of 8 October 2001 relating to the involvement of employees, a special negotiating body (SNB) is formed by elected employees representatives or by representatives appointed by unions. The SNB and the management of the SE must enter into a written agreement which will set out the terms and conditions of the involvement of employees within the SE, including representation, information and consultation procedure and rules for board-level participation. In SE established by transformation, the agreement must provide for at least the same level of employee involvement as existed within the company being transformed. If no agreement is reached, or the parties so decide, a statutory set of 'standard rules' applies providing for a standard 'representative body'.

[165] Pursuant to Article 69 of the EC Regulation No. 2157/2001, on 19 November 2010, the Commission has presented a report on the application of the Regulation related to the SE to the Council and the European Parliament and made proposals for amendments.

[166] Furthermore, the European Commission has presented in June 2008 a proposal for a Statute on a European Private Company ('Societas Privata Europaea' – 'SPE'). This new company form will enable small- and medium-sized enterprises

(SME) to do business throughout the EU, with the aim of cutting costs and encouraging growth in this area. At the same time, it will benefit larger groups in organizing their subsidiaries abroad.

[167] The SPE has been designed to address the current onerous obligations on SME operating across borders, which need to set up subsidiaries in different company forms in every Member State in which they want to do business. In practical terms, the SPE would mean that SME can set up their company in the same form, no matter if they do business in their own Member State or in another. Opting for the SPE will save entrepreneurs time and money on legal advice, management and administration. The proposal is still being discussed before the European Parliament and the Council.

Other Types of Corporate Structures

Groupement d'Intérêt Economique (GIE)

[168] The Economic Interest Grouping or GIE is governed by Articles L.251-1 to L.251-23 of the French Commercial Code, which aims to enable companies to pool their resources while remaining independent. It is a legal entity with at least two members, which is distinct from its members, although it is not a company. The members may be French or foreign individuals or legal entities.

[169] A GIE must carry out an economic activity which may be either civil or commercial. The GIE activity must be an extension of and ancillary to the activity of its members, which restricts significantly the use of this structure for joint ventures.

[170] A GIE is not intended to make profits per se, although it may make such profits in the normal course of its business. There is no capital requirement. However, a GIE may receive contributions in cash or in kind from its members. A GIE may issue bonds if all its members are companies authorized to issue bonds.

[171] It can be managed either by individuals or by legal entities which must appoint an individual as permanent representative. The members can freely determine in the articles of association the number of directors, the way they will be appointed, their terms of office and the conditions for their appointment and removal. The directors are jointly and severally liable if they commit any fault in the management of the GIE or if they do not comply with the articles of association or the legal provisions which regulate GIE's.

[172] The members have the greatest flexibility to organize within the articles of association the rules relating to general members' meetings (scope of authority, majority, quorum, etc.) as well as the rules regarding the appointment and power of the GIE's controller. Unless otherwise provided in the articles of association, the unanimous consent of the members is required for the acceptance of new members.

[173] The GIE is a flexible structure, and there are no cumbersome formalities with respect to its creation or operation. The fiscal transparency of the GIE is an additional tax advantage. One of the most notable companies which have chosen this form is Airbus Industries. However, the GIE is not as commonly used as it could be in the context of joint ventures for a number of reasons:

(i) its members are jointly and severally liable for the GIE's debts (the GIE may nevertheless ask the contractor to waive the members' liability and agree only to pursue the group itself); (ii) should the GIE be declared bankrupt, the bankruptcy would then be extended to all its members; and (iii) the activity of the GIE must be ancillary to the activity of its members and can neither be substituted for this activity nor be a new one.

[174] A structure which is quite similar to the GIE, the European Economic Interest Grouping (EEIG) provided by the Council regulation (EEC) N°2137/85 of 25 July 1985 can be registered in France. The EEIG is governed by Articles L.252-1 to L.252-13 of the French Commercial Code.

Société en Participation

[175] A *société en participation* is similar to a silent partnership. It is not a legal entity and is therefore not subject to any registration formalities. It can be deemed to be either of a commercial or civil nature, depending on its activity. Its existence should, in principle, remain unknown to third parties. Partners may agree not to disclose the *société en participation* to anybody except the tax authorities: such *société en participation* files tax returns like any *société civile* or SNC according to the civil or commercial nature of its activity.

[176] In such a case, only the active partner commits himself or herself *vis-à-vis* third parties. However, in the case of deficiency, the 'silent partner' would be called upon by the active partner to contribute his or her share of the losses incurred. It is generally felt that third parties can take no action against silent partners if the existence of the *société en participation* is not disclosed. The main advantages of this kind of arrangement are its flexibility and its confidentiality.

Sociétés de Participations Financières de Professions Libérales (SPFPL)

[177] SPFPL have a special corporate purpose which is to hold shares of a *société d'exercice libéral*.

[178] A SPFPL is a pure holding company. It cannot exercise in a liberal profession by itself. However, SPFPL may exercise incidental activities related to their main one.

[179] SPFPL are composed of individuals or legal persons exercising a liberal profession. Legal persons could belong to several forms of French companies (sociétés civiles, sociétés commerciales, sociétés coopératives). More than the half of the equity and the voting rights must be held by individuals or legal persons exercising the same profession as the owned companies.

[180] A SPFPL can be incorporated in the form of a SARL, SAS, SAS or SCA.

[181] The corporate name of the company must be preceded or followed by the mention *Société de participations financiers de professions libérale*.

Rights of Minority Shareholders

[182] One of the principals governing French corporate law is the one according to which shareholders are equal, and that each share shall grant his or her holder with similar rights and obligations to those of other shareholders. However, discrimination may be authorized by law, and result from different classes or categories of shares set by the articles of association (within the same class or category, shareholders shall be equal). However, where an investor acquires less than 100% of the share capital of a company, his rights to influence the decision-making process in the company depend on his level of participation as well as on the legal form of the company. Furthermore, French company law provides for some protection of minority shareholders, and such protection is reinforced for minority shareholders of listed companies. In private companies, rights or protection may also be validly granted to minority shareholders by shareholders agreements (drag along clause, pre-emptive rights, rights to propose Board members, financial reporting, etc.).

[183] Abuse of majority voting rights or abuse of minority voting rights, that is, the repeated or unjustified exercise by either a majority shareholder or a minority shareholder of his or her voting rights, may entail the invalidity of the vote of such shareholder if it can be proved to a court that the shareholder was acting in his or her own personal interest and against the interests of the company. The shareholder convicted of abuse of right may also be held liable for damages to the other shareholders.

Minority Shareholders' Rights and Protection in *Sociétés de Capitaux* (SA or SCA) or in the SARL

[184] In contrast to other *Sociétés de Capitaux*, the rights of minority shareholders of an SAS depend solely on the majority rules set by the articles of association (except for those resolutions requiring the unanimous consent of the shareholders by virtue of the law as referred to above).

Shareholders Holding at Least 75% of the Share Capital

[185] A shareholder, provided he or she holds at least 75% of the shares of an SARL, may decide for all shareholders decisions except when a unanimous consent of the shareholders is required by the law.

Shareholders Holding Over 50% of the Share Capital

[186] A shareholder holding just over 50% of the voting rights of an SA or an SCA or an SARL may control shareholder's decisions and actions which require for their validity the prior authorization of an ordinary general meeting of shareholders. Such decisions include the following, among others:

- approval of the accounts of the previous fiscal year,
- appointment of new Board members,

- approval of agreements entered into, directly or indirectly, between the company and Board members or shareholders holding more than 10% of the share capital.

Minority Shareholders Holding over One Third or 25% of the Voting Rights

[187] A minority shareholder holding just over one third of the voting rights of an SA or an SCA or 25% of the voting rights of an SARL (except when the articles of association of the SARL set a majority for the extraordinary shareholders meeting less than 75% of the shares), may veto decisions and actions which require for their validity the prior authorization of an extraordinary general meeting of shareholders. Such decisions include the following:

- all amendments to the articles of association of the company (in particular any increase or reduction of the share capital, any transfer of the registered office except within the same area, any change in the company's purpose, any change in the number of directors, any inclusion of or amendment to clauses restricting transfers of shares);
- acts of disposal or transfer of the business of the company or of its major assets or a substantial part of the company's assets;
- merger transactions and partial transfers of business in consideration for shares of another company;
- approval of the transfer of shares in the company to non-shareholders (in the case of an SARL);
- issue of convertible bonds;
- transformation of the legal form of the company.

[188] With 25% of the voting rights of an SA, by attending an extraordinary shareholders' meeting, a minority shareholder can make certain that the quorum is met on first call.

Minority Shareholders Holding Over 20% of the Share Capital

[189] With 20% of the voting rights of an SA, by attending a shareholders' meeting a minority shareholder can make certain that the quorum is met on second call for an extraordinary general meeting and on first call for an ordinary general meeting.

Minority Shareholders Holding Over 10% of the Share Capital

[190] A minority shareholder who holds at least 10% of the share capital of a *société commerciale* can require the establishment of consolidated accounts if the statutory conditions are met even in the event the company is itself under the control of another company and is included as such in the consolidated accounts of such company.

Article 6. Minority Shareholders Holding over 5% of the Share Capital

[191] A minority shareholder who holds at least 5% of the share capital of an SA, SCA or SARL can exercise the following rights:

- to request that a draft resolution be added to the agenda and be addressed by the next shareholders meeting;
- cause the appointment of a judicial agent (*mandataire judiciaire*) to convene a general shareholders' meeting (irrespective of the size of his or her shareholding in the case of shareholders of an SARL) provided the request complies with the company's interests;
- submit twice a year written questions to the Board or to the *gérant* on facts which may jeopardize the company's business (irrespective of the size of his or her shareholding in the case of shareholders of an SARL);
- require dismissal or judicial revocation of the company's statutory auditor (or in the case of an SARL which does not satisfy the statutory conditions to appoint a statutory auditor, require the appointment by the Commercial Court of a statutory auditor);
- cause a judicial investigator (*expert judiciaire*) to be appointed by the court in order to review and appraise certain actions or decisions of the management of the company. This is in general a way of obtaining clear evidence of mismanagement with a view to an action in damages against the director or the *gérant*;
- to exercise on his or her own behalf and on behalf of other minority shareholders (if they together own not less than 5% of the share capital) the so-called *action sociale*. Where the share capital of an SA or SCA exceeds EUR750,000, the minimum percentage is reduced to 4% up to EUR750,000, plus 2.5% for the part of the share capital which ranges between EUR750,000 and EUR7.5 million, then 1% between EUR7.5 million and EUR15 million and 0.50% over EUR15 million.

[192] A minority shareholder of an SAS who holds at least 5% of the share capital can also exercise certain of the above-mentioned rights such as to require the dismissal or judicial revocation of the company's statutory auditor, to submit twice a year written questions to the president on facts which may jeopardize the company's business or to cause a judicial investigator to be appointed by the court in order to review and appraise certain actions or decisions of the management of the company.

[193] With respect to the other rights available to shareholders of an SA pursuant to French law, the shareholders of an SAS cannot avail themselves of such rights, as the statutory provisions applicable to the SA do not apply to the SAS. However, the articles of association of the SAS can always grant to the shareholders certain rights. Furthermore, the following decisions must be passed unanimously by the shareholders of an SAS: additions to the articles of association or amendment of the articles of association regarding restrictions on the transfer of shares; approval of transfers of shares; and the exclusion of a corporate shareholder in case of change of control.

Minority Shareholders Holding at Least One Share

[194] Ultimately a minority shareholder holding at least a single share in the share capital of an SA, SCA or SARL has the right to attend the general meetings, to have the mandatory information available at the registered office or sent to him or her before the general meetings, to ask written questions to the Board or to the *gérant* during the period preceding the shareholders' meeting. He or she may also cause the appointment of a judicial agent to convene a general shareholders' meeting (for the SA or the SCA in case of urgency only) or obtain from the court an order cancelling a decision which was in the exclusive interest of the majority shareholders but contrary to the interest of the company and to the detriment of the minority shareholders. Furthermore, the minority shareholder of an SA, an SCA, an SAS or an SARL may veto decisions and actions which require for their validity the unanimous consent of shareholders such as: the change in the nationality of the company; the transformation of the company into another corporate form resulting in unlimited liability for shareholders, or any increase of liability of the shareholders including a share capital increase by increase of the per value of the shares except in the event of share capital increase by incorporation of reserves.

[195] A shareholder may also, regardless of the size of his or her shareholding, require the court to appoint a judicial administrator who will manage the company in lieu of the existing management. However, such an action will be successful only in cases where specific circumstances evidence the fact that the day-to-day management of the company has been rendered impossible, for example by reason of a deadlock at the Board of Directors or a misuse by the majority shareholders of their rights so as to jeopardize the company's interests.

[196] In practice the courts are rather reluctant to appoint a judicial administrator when the company's interests are not jeopardized over a short time period. However, French courts may, when the company's interests seem to be at risk and when there appears to be a fundamental disagreement between the shareholders, decide to prohibit the company's directors over a specific period from doing any managerial act which may have irrevocable consequences for the company and at the same time to appoint a judicial agent (*mandataire de justice*) to attend shareholders' meetings or the Board of Directors' meetings with a view to supervising any failure to comply with such prohibition.

Article 8. Minority Shareholders' Protection in Listed Companies

[197] In addition to the rights referred to above, special protection is granted to minority shareholders of a company whose shares are listed on a regulated market (meaning that those traded on the *Marché libre* are exempted). A minority shareholder, regardless of the size of his or her shareholding in the listed company, may require the *Autorité des Marchés Financiers* (AMF) to cause the majority shareholders to submit a public offer to purchase the shares held by the minority shareholders under an *offre de retrait* (squeeze out). This procedure enables the minority shareholders to withdraw from a listed company, especially when the market is no longer liquid as a result of the prevailing position of one or several shareholders holding at least 95% of the voting rights in the general meeting.

[198] Furthermore, protection of minority shareholders in companies with shares listed on a regulated market (Euronext) or an organized market (Alternext), is ensured through the increased financial information required by the French company law or the AMF General regulation (including transpositions of EC Directives) to be made available to the public (including the minority shareholders) at the registered office (free of charge), on the companies dedicated website and in the *Bulletin des Annonces Légales et Obligatoires* (BALO), a special legal gazette.

[199] The annual financial reports which include the annual accounts, where applicable, the consolidated accounts prepared in accordance with Regulation (EC) 1606/2002 of 19 July 2002 on the application of international accounting standards, a management report, a statement made by the natural persons taking responsibility for the annual financial report, whose names and functions must be clearly indicated, to the effect that, to the best of their knowledge. The accounts are prepared in accordance with the applicable set of accounting standards and give a true and fair view of the assets, liabilities financial position and profit or loss of the issuer and the undertakings in the consolidation taken as a whole, and that the management report includes a fair review of the development and performance of the business, profit or loss and financial position of the issuer and the undertakings in the consolidation taken as a whole, together with a description of the principal risks and uncertainties that they face, the report of the statutory auditors on the annual accounts and, where applicable, the consolidated accounts. Furthermore, the annual financial report may include the news release concerning the statutory auditors' fees. In this case, this information is not published separately.

[200] The half-yearly financial report which includes complete or condensed accounts for the past half-year, in consolidated form where necessary, an interim management report, a statement made by the natural persons taking responsibility for the half-yearly financial report, to the effect that, to the best of their knowledge, the accounts are prepared in accordance with the applicable set of accounting standards and give a true and fair view of the assets, liabilities, financial position and profit or loss of the issuer and the undertakings in the consolidation taken as a whole, the statutory auditors' report on the limited review of the aforementioned accounts. The interim management report shall describe the material events that occurred in the first six months of the financial year and their impact on the interim accounts, the principal risks and uncertainties for the remaining six months of the year.

[201] Within forty-five days of the first and third quarters of their fiscal year, the issuer shall publish quarterly financial reports, detailing the main transactions and events which took place during the period in question and their impact on the financial situation of the issuer and the entities it controls; the financial situation and results of the issuer and the entities it controls during the period in question; and the net amount of turnover for the last quarter per economic sector and, where applicable, for each of the preceding quarters of the current accounting period and for the period as a whole, together with an indication of the corresponding turnover figures for the previous accounting period (established on an individual or consolidated basis, as applicable).

[202] Within twenty days of distributing the annual financial report, listed companies shall file electronically with the AMF a document containing or mentioning all the information they have published or made public over the previous twelve months in one or more States party to the EEA agreement or in one or more third countries in order to fulfil their legal or regulatory obligations with respect to financial instruments, financial instrument issuers and financial instrument markets.

[203] Within four months of the end of their financial year, listed companies shall publish a news release specifying the fees paid to each of the statutory auditors responsible for auditing their financial statements and, where applicable, to the company through which those auditors carry out their duties, or to other professionals in the network to which that company belongs, wherever such network, composed of natural or legal persons, provides professional services or advice in accounting, financial statement auditing, non-statutory auditing, or consulting on legal, financial, tax, organizational or related matters, and directly or indirectly maintains relations within the network that establishes a material and durable community of economic interest.

[204] [Pursuant to AMF Regulation, information provided to the public must be accurate, precise and fairly presented. Any significant fact which may have an impact on the value of listed shares must be disclosed to the public as soon as possible except when the publication of such information might have a negative effect on the company's legitimate interests; in such a case the company may decide to postpone publication for confidentiality purposes provided the company is able to keep such information confidential and that such non-disclosure is unlikely to mislead the public.

[205] Any person preparing to implement a financial transaction likely to have a significant impact on the value of the listed shares must as soon as possible inform the public of the nature of such transaction unless publication thereof is postponed for confidentiality reasons by the relevant persons.

[206] The AMF may request companies to publicly disclose, in a timely fashion, information that the AMF deems necessary for investor protection and orderly markets. Failing such publication, the AMF itself may disclose the information.

[207] Are also requested to be disclosed to the public crossing of shareholding thresholds, declarations of intent and changes of intent, information about the total number of voting rights and shares making up the share capital, shareholder agreements, information on proposals to amend the articles of association, transactions in the company's securities by officers and directors and statement of intent in the event of preparations for a takeover bid.

Minority Partners of *Sociétés de Personnes* or of *Sociétés Civiles*

[208] The protection of the minority partners of *sociétés de personnes* or of *sociétés civiles* depends on the provision of the articles of association, since most resolutions are passed with the unanimous consent of the partners except as otherwise provided in the articles of association (except for those resolutions requiring the unanimous consent of the shareholders by virtue of the law as referred to above).

[209] A minority shareholder, regardless of the size of his or her shareholding, has the following rights:

- he or she may require the judicial dismissal of the *gérant* provided he or she can prove there are legitimate grounds for such dismissal;
- he or she may also require the president of the Commercial Court or of a Civil Court to order the judicial liquidation of the company or to exercise an *action sociale* against the management.

Minority Shareholder and the *'Action Sociale'* or *'Action ut Singuli'*

[210] The *action sociale* is a tort action against the management which is exercised on behalf of the company by a shareholder or a group of shareholders. The action will result in damages being awarded to the company (and not to the shareholder) if successful. It is necessary to prove the loss incurred by the company and the fault or negligence of the management.

[211] The *action sociale* should be distinguished from the individual and separate action of a shareholder or third party against the management and which aims at compensating the plaintiff for individual loss allegedly suffered.

[212] A minority shareholder of a *société de capitaux* and of an SARL may go to the courts to initiate an *action sociale* on his or her own behalf and on behalf of other minority shareholders if they together own at least 5% of the share capital (except for the *société par actions* when the capital is over EUR750,000 as described above). It should be noted that the *action sociale* may also be initiated individually by any minority shareholder of a *société commerciale* irrespective of the shareholding. The shareholder of the SNC can only exercise the *action sociale* individually.

REGULATORY AND OTHER AUTHORIZATIONS

Foreign Investment Regulations

Overview

[213] Foreign investment controls have been significantly lifted in France. Pursuant to Articles L.151-1 to L.151-4 and R.151-1 to R.153-12 of the French Financial and Monetary Code (*Code Monétaire et Financier*) (as amended by Law 2004-1343 dated 9 December 2004, Decree 2005-1739 dated 30 December 2005, Decree 2010-1011 dated 30 August 2010, Decree 2012-1182 dated 23 October 2012, Decree 2012-691 dated 7 May 2012, and Decree 2013-383 dated 6 May 2013), and the *arrêté* dated 7 March 2003, a foreign direct investment in France made by non-French residing investors is merely subject to an administrative declaration to be made to the Treasury Department at the Ministry of Economy and Finance simultaneously with the completion of the investment. However, foreign investments in a business activity in France which, even on an occasional basis, participates in the exercise of public authority are subject to prior authorization of the Ministry of Economy and Finance. (*Ministère de l'Economie, des Finances et de l'Emploi, Direction Générale du Trésor et de la Politique Economique (DGTPE), Multicom 2, 139 rue de Bercy, 75572 Paris cedex 12 (tel. 33- (0)1.44.87.72.87)*:

[214] According to Article R.151-1 of the French Financial and Monetary Code (*Code Monétaire et Financier*), 'Non-French Residing Investors' include individuals who do not principally reside in France, foreign civil servants or agents of other states residing in France for their office, and legal entities registered outside of France.

[215] 'France' means, according to the Article R.151-1, the French metropolitan territory (which includes Corsica), French Western Indies (Guadeloupe, Guyane, Martinique), Reunion Island, Mayotte, Wallis and Futuna Islands, St Pierre-et-Miquelon and also the Principality of Monaco. Nevertheless, Wallis and Futuna is not considered as 'France' for statistics related to balance of payments studies.

Foreign Investments Subject to Administrative Declaration to the Ministry of Economy and Finance

[216] According to Articles R.151-1 and R.151-5 of the French Financial and Monetary Code (*Code Monétaire et Financier*), the following foreign investments, which are qualified as 'direct', require only an administrative declaration to the Treasury Department at the Ministry of Economy and Finance at the time of completion of the first investment:

- the setting-up of a new company by a foreign company or a non resident individual;
- the acquisition of all or part of a business line of a French company by a foreign company or by a non-resident individual;
- all transactions carried out in the share capital of a French company by a foreign company or a non-resident individual as soon as, following the relevant transaction, the cumulated amount of the capital or voting rights held by foreign companies or non-resident individuals exceeds 33.33% of the capital or voting rights of the French company;
- the same transactions carried out by a French company, the capital or voting rights of which are held more than 33.33% by one or several foreign companies or by one or several non-resident individuals;
- transactions such as the granting of loans or substantial guarantees or the purchase of patents or licenses, the acquisition of commercial contracts or the provision of technical assistance entailing the de facto takeover of a French company by a foreign company or by a non-resident individual;
- transactions carried out abroad, the effect of which is to modify the control of a non-resident company that itself holds an equity interest or voting rights in a French company, the capital or voting rights of which are held at more than 33.33% by one or several foreign companies or by non-resident individuals.

[217] However, the following transactions are exempted from the declaration formality (unless it relates to a regulated activity):

- the creation or extension of business activity of a French company held directly or indirectly by foreign companies or by non-resident individuals;
- an increase in shareholding of a French company held directly or indirectly by foreign companies or by non-resident individuals, if the increase is carried out by an investor already holding more than 50% of the capital or voting rights of the company;
- the subscription to a share capital increase of a French company held directly or indirectly by foreign companies or by non-resident individuals if they do not increase their proportionate shareholding;
- direct investments carried out between companies that all belong to the same group; i.e., which are held directly or indirectly at more than 50% by the same shareholders;
- transactions relating to loans, advances, guarantees, consolidations or discharge of indebtedness, subsidies, or *dotation de succursales* granted by a French company held directly or indirectly by foreign companies or by non-resident individuals;
- direct investments in French companies carrying out a real estate business other than the construction of buildings intended to be sold or leased;
- direct investments, within the limit of EUR1.5 million, in French small-scale, retail, hotel, catering, or convenience services companies or companies the sole purpose of which is the exploitation of quarry or gravel pit;
- acquisitions of agricultural land.

[218] Pursuant to sections R. 152-1 to R.152-4 of the French Financial and Monetary Code (*Code Monétaire et Financier*), some investments which are exempted from a declaration are nonetheless subject to 'statistical declarations' in view of drawing up French balance of trade and external position statistics, such as:

- the creation or extension of business activity of a French company held directly or indirectly by foreign companies or by non-resident individuals;
- direct investments carried out in French companies performing a real estate business when these investments exceed EUR1.5 million;
- the acquisitions of viticultural land.

Foreign Investments Subject to Prior Authorization of the Ministry of Economy and Finance

[219] Foreign investments in a business activity in France which, even on an occasional basis, participates in the exercise of public authority or falls within the scope of one of the following areas are subject to prior authorization: business activities likely to be detrimental to public policy, the public safety or the interest of national defence or business activities in the field of research, production or commercialization of weapons, munitions, gun powder and explosive substances, or security systems, among others.

[220] Prior to carrying out an investment, it is possible to submit a written request to the Minister in Charge of Economic Affairs to know whether or not the investment is subject to the authorization process. The Minister must answer within a period of two months. However, the absence of an answer is not deemed to be an exemption from the authorization request.

[221] In addition to the general rules described above, it is necessary to draw a distinction depending on whether the relevant investment comes from a third country or from a Member State of the EU.

[222] Provisions relating to foreign investments coming from third countries: Investments carried out (i) by an individual who is not a citizen of a Member State of the EU or of a State that is party to the European Economic Area having entered into an administrative assistance agreement with France or (ii) by a company, the registered office of which is not located in one of these States, or (iii) by an individual who is a French national but is not a resident of one of these States fall within the scope of the prior authorization regime when they concern the business activities referred to in section R.153-2 of the French Financial and Monetary Code. For purposes of the application of these provisions, an investment is considered to include the investor either (i) acquiring the control, within the meaning of section L.233-3 of the French Code de commerce, of a company, the registered office of which is located in France; or (ii) acquiring, directly or indirectly, all or part of a business line of a company, the registered office of which is located in France; or (iii) crossing the threshold of 33.33% of direct or indirect holding of the share capital and voting rights of a company, the registered office of which is located in France.

[223] Provisions relating to foreign investments coming from Member States of the EU. Pursuant to Articles R153-4 and R153-5-2 of the French Financial and Monetary Code, the investments carried out by (i) an individual who is a citizen of a Member State of the EUor of a State that is party to the European Economic Area having entered into an administrative assistance agreement with France or by a company, the registered office of which is located in one of these States or by an individual who is a French national who is a resident in one of these States, or (ii) the investments carried out by a French company controlled (within the meaning of section L.233-3 of the French Code de Commerce) by an foreign individual or by a Company registered aboard or by an French individual who is a citizen aboard fall within the scope of the prior authorization regime when they concern the business activities referred to in 8 to 11 of section R.153-2 of the French Financial and Monetary Code and section R.153-5 of the French Financial and Monetary Code.

[224] For the purposes of the application of these provisions, shall be considered as an investment the fact for the investor of either acquiring the control, within the meaning of section L.233-3 of the French Commercial Code, of a company, the registered office of which is located in France, or acquiring, directly or indirectly, all or part of a business line of a company, the registered office of which is located in France.

[225] The Ministry of Economy and Finance shall render his or her decision within two months following the date of receipt of the authorization request, failing which, the authorization shall be deemed to be obtained. The authorization that is granted may, however, be paired, as the case may be, with conditions intended to ensure that the contemplated investment will not be prejudicial to national interests.

[226] Exceptions: The authorization is deemed to be obtained when the foreign investment is carried out in companies that all belong to the same group, i.e., more than 50% of their capital and voting rights is held, directly or indirectly, by the same shareholder, except where the purpose of the investment is to transfer abroad all or part of a business line of one of the activities listed in section R.153-2 and R.153-4 of the French Financial and Monetary Code.

[227] If the Ministry of Economy and Finance establishes that a foreign investment is or has been carried out in disregard for the aforementioned rules, he or she may require the investor not to pursue the transaction, to modify it or to have, at the investor's expenses, the initial situation restored. This injunction may only occur following the transmission of a formal notice to the investor inviting the investor to present its comments within fifteen days.

[228] Pursuant to Article R153-10 of the French Financial and Monetary Code, the Ministry of Economy and Finance shall refuse by reasoned decision the project of investment if (i) there is a serious presumption the investor may commit an offence according to French Penal Code, or (ii) provisions of Article R153-9 of the French Financial and Monetary Code are not sufficient to preserve national interests.

[229] In the case of non-compliance, the Ministry of Economy and Finance may, *inter alia*, without prejudice to the restoration of the previous situation, impose a fine on the investor, the maximum amount of which shall be equal to twice the amount of the irregular investment. The sanction must, however, be proportional to the gravity of the breaches that have been committed.

Status of Foreign Businessmen in France

[230] The former Foreign Business Card (*carte d'identité de commerçant étranger*) required from foreign individuals to operate businesses in France was abrogated in May 2007 and a new set of rules was established by decrees dated 9 May 2007, 15 May 2007 and 26 July 2007 (Articles L.122-1 and D.122-1 to D.122-4 of the Commercial Code, and l.121-1 and L121-1 of the Foreign citizens code (*Code des étrangers*)).

[231] A natural person who is not a French citizen or a citizen of a Member State of the EU, of Switzerland, of Norway, of Liechtenstein or of Iceland, is subject to a special regulation to take one of the following offices in a company in France:

- partner liable for the corporate debts to an unlimited extent in an SNC, SCS or SCA;
- *gérant* in an SARL;
- president of the Board of Directors or general manager of an SA;

- president of an SAS;
- president of directorate (*Directoire*) or general manager of an SA with the structure of directorate and Supervisory Board;
- director of a GIE;
- legal representative of a branch.

[232] A distinction is to be made between persons who will reside in France for their office and persons who are not required to reside in France for their office.

[233] To reside in France: according to the Foreign citizens code (*Code des étrangers*), any foreigner must hold a resident permit authorizing him or her to reside in France and to exercise such a professional activity in France.

[234] An application must be filed with the French Consulate in the country where the foreigner is residing, or if he or she already has a French resident permit but which does not allow him or her to have such a position in France, the application is to be filed with the local French authorities (*préfecture*) within the jurisdiction in which he or she resides.

[235] When the foreign individual will not reside in France, he or she must make a declaration to the local French authorities (*préfecture*) within the jurisdiction in which the company is located prior to the registration of his or her office with the Trade and Companies Registry. This declaration is made by registered letter and must enclose the articles of association of the company, information on the civil status of the applicant and a copy of his or her criminal record. The *préfet* acknowledges receipt which is required by the Trade and Companies Registry for the registration of the office of the applicant. This matter is regulated by the Commercial Code.

[236] Pursuant to Article L122-2 of the French commercial code, any breach of the provisions for foreign individuals to operate business in France shall be punished by a fine of EUR3,750 and six months of prison.

Antitrust Regulations

Merger Control

[237] Investments in France may be subject to European Commission merger control or French authorities merger control.

European Merger Control

[238] Merger control in the EU is under the responsibility of the European Commission. Under European law, a concentration is defined as a merger between previously independent companies, an acquisition of direct or indirect control over the whole or part of another company, or the creation of a fully-functional joint venture. The transaction cannot be implemented before the approval of the Commission.

[239] A concentration has a community dimension (e.g., mandatory control of the EU Commission) where the following conditions are fulfilled:

- the combined aggregate worldwide turnover of all the undertakings concerned is more than EUR5 billion; and
- the aggregate Community-wide turnover of each of at least two of the undertakings concerned is more than EUR250 million, unless each of the undertakings concerned achieves more than two thirds of its aggregate Community-wide turnover within one and the same Member State.

[240] a concentration that does not meet the aforementioned thresholds shall nonetheless be deemed to have a Community dimension, and thus be notified, where all of the following criteria are met:

- the combined aggregate worldwide turnover of all the undertakings concerned is more than EUR2.5 billion;
- in each of at least three Member States, the combined aggregate turnover of all the undertakings concerned is more than EUR100 million;
- in each of at least three Member States, the aggregate turnover of each of at least two of the undertakings concerned is more than EUR25 million; and
- the aggregate Community-wide turnover of each of at least two of the undertakings concerned is more than EUR100 million, unless each of the undertakings concerned achieves more than two thirds of its aggregate Community-wide turnover within one and the same Member State.

[241] A concentration with a Community dimension shall be notified to the Commission prior to its implementation and following the conclusion of the agreement, the announcement of the public bid, or the acquisition of a controlling interest. The notification procedure may comprise two phases:

- *Phase I*: where the European Commission finds that the concentration would not significantly impede effective competition in the common market and, therefore, decides not to oppose it, it shall, within twenty-five working days after the date of filing (thirty-five working days if the parties offer commitments), declare the transaction compatible with the Common Market;
- *Phase II*: where the European Commission finds that the concentration would significantly impede effective competition in the Common Market, it will initiate proceedings. The European Commission then has a ninety working day period to make a final decision authorizing (with or without conditions) or opposing the concentration. This period may be extended (up to twenty working days) if the notifying parties make a request to that effect and shall be increased to 105 working days where the undertakings concerned offer commitments.

French Merger Control

[242] Merger control in France is under the responsibility of the French Competition Authority (*Autorité de la Concurrence*) and of the Ministry of Economy (*Ministre de l'Economie, des Finances et de l'Emploi*). French merger control provides for a mandatory filing for transactions which fulfil the following criteria:

- the transaction is a concentration (the French definition being similar to the European one);
- since 29 March 2011 the transaction must meet the thresholds provided by Article L430-2 of the French Commercial Code: the aggregate worldwide turnover of all the companies parties to the transaction exceeds EUR150 million, each of at least two parties to the transaction achieved a turnover in France exceeding EUR50 million and the transaction does not have a Community dimension (if it does, it should be notified to the European Commission). The thresholds are different if the concentration concerns retail stores.

[243] A concentration shall be notified to the Competition Authority before the signing of a binding agreement provided that the parties have agreed to the main terms of the transaction. There is no mandatory filing period. However a concentration cannot be implemented prior to a clearance decision of the Competition Authority. Should the party(ies) vested with the obligation to notify fail to file a reportable concentration or implement it prior to a clearance decision, the party(ies) will be liable to a fine up to 5% of the turnover achieved in France for the last financial year.

[244] The notification procedure comprises two phases:

- Phase 1: should the Ministry of Economy consider that the concentration does not raise any competition concerns, it will issue an express or tacit clearance decision within five weeks (or eight weeks if the parties offer commitments);
- Phase 2: should the Ministry of Economy consider that the concentration raises serious competition concerns, it will request a formal opinion from the Competition Authority, which must render a non-binding decision within three months. The Ministry then has four weeks to make its final decision on the case. This decision can be appealed before the French administrative Supreme Court.

Cartel Regulation

[245] Article 101 of the FEU Treaty of the Functioning of the European Union (FUE) and Article L.420-1 of the French Commercial Code prohibit anti-competitive agreements, especially agreements to fix prices, share markets, share commercially sensitive information, restrict output or apply dissimilar conditions to equivalent transactions. Cartels are prohibited per se, which means that demonstration of an effect on competition is not necessary.

European Cartel Regulation

[246] Article 101 provides that any agreement, decision or concerted practice between companies which may affect trade between Member States and which have as their object or effect the prevention, restriction or distortion of competition are prohibited. As a matter of practice, any agreement which fixes prices, limits outputs, shares markets, customers or sources of supply or involves other cartel behaviour will almost inevitably be regarded as restricting competition. According to the

Commission, these types of agreement constitute 'hard-core' restrictions and may be presumed to have negative effects.

[247] It should be emphasized that the Commission considers that if parties' cumulative market shares do not exceed 10% on any of the relevant markets on which the parties are active (the threshold will be 15% if the parties are not present on the same market(s) or potential competitors), the agreement does not appreciably restrict competition.

[248] According to Regulation 1/2003, agreements which satisfy the conditions of Article 101 (3) are not prohibited, no prior decision to that effect being required. This requires that:

- the agreements contribute to improving the production or distribution of goods or to promoting technical or economic progress, while allowing consumers a fair share of the resulting benefit;
- the agreements do not impose on the undertakings concerned restrictions which are not indispensable to the attainment of these objectives and afford such undertakings the possibility of eliminating competition in respect of a substantial part of the products in question.

[249] It should nevertheless be emphasized that a hard-core agreement cannot be qualified as an exemption under Article 101(3). The Commission's principal powers of investigation are to require companies to provide information, to conduct dawn raids at company premises and to inspect employees' homes and cars, etc., and to take statements from individuals or legal entities.

[250] Where the Commission considers that a company has infringed Article 101, the agreement is void and the Commission imposes fines, which may not exceed 10% of total turnover in the preceding business year, and the amount of which depends on the gravity and the duration of the infringement. The Commission's decisions can be appealed to the EU Court of First Instance, which has jurisdiction to review the legality of and reasons for the decisions and their procedural propriety and to assess the appropriateness of the amount of the fines.

[251] The Commission also applies a leniency programme based on two main principles. First, the earlier companies contact the Commission, the higher the reward is: full immunity is granted either to the first company to provide the Commission with sufficient evidence to enable the Commission to take a decision to carry out a dawn raid, or to the first company to submit evidence enabling the Commission to find infringement of Article 101. Secondly, the reward will depend on the usefulness of the materials supplied. Favourable treatment is also available to companies that do not qualify for immunity but provide evidence contributing 'significant added value' to what the Commission already has.

French Cartel Regulation

[252] In France, cartel law can be influenced by various authorities and courts (French Competition Authority or any civil, criminal or administrative court).They are competent to apply both Article L. 420-1 of the French Commercial Code and

Article 101 of the FEU Treaty. However where the investigated cartel affects trade between Member States, the Competition Authority(*Autorité de la Concurrence*) or the court must apply Article 101. Moreover the application of national law must not lead to the prohibition of agreements which may affect trade between Member States but which are valid under European competition law.

[253] Article L.420-1 of the Code prohibits cartels and concerted practices in a similar way to Article 101(1) of the FEU Treaty. The Competition Authority must produce evidence demonstrating that the parallel behaviour is the result of the parties' intention not to act independently from each other. The burden of proof is on the Competition Authority.

[254] The Competition Authority is authorized to take a non-suit decision if the parties' cumulative market shares do not exceed 15% on any of the relevant markets affected by the agreement (30% if the parties are not present or potential competitors). As for European Union law (EU law), this exemption does not apply to the most serious cartels (price-fixing, market-sharing, etc.). Article L.420-4 also organizes, under French law, an exemption system, quite similar to the one provided for under EU law.

[255] The investigation may start after a complaint is filed before the Competition Authority. The Competition Authority may also take up a matter on its own initiative, or after a decision of the Ministry of Economy. Investigations may be carried out by the DGCCRF (a service of the Ministry of Economy) or the Competition Authority. As for EU law, the powers of investigation granted to the DGCCRF or the Competition Authority are very broad.

[256] Where the Competition Authority considers that an undertaking has infringed article L. 420-1 or Article 101, the agreement is void and the Competition Authority imposes fines, the amount of which may not exceed 10% of their consolidated pre-tax turnover worldwide. The Competition Authority may also order periodic penalty payments up to 5% of the average daily turnover of a company, in order to compel it to bring the infringement to an end, to comply with a decision, or to comply with a binding commitment. The Competition Authority's decisions are subject to appeal before the Paris Court of Appeal, whose decisions may be challenged before the Supreme Court.

[257] Similar to the Commission, the Competition Authority also applies a leniency programme. First, a total or partial exoneration may be granted to an undertaking which has carried out a prohibited practice; it contributes to establishing the reality of the prohibited practice and to identifying its perpetrators, by providing information which the Competition Authority or the French administration (DGCCRF) did not have previously. Secondly, the exoneration is proportionate to the contribution made to establishing the offence. There is no legal 'immunity plus' programme: going second may give the authority access to information that it did not have, although normally to a lesser extent than that provided by the first in.

Abuse of Dominant Position

[258] Article 102 of the FEU Treaty and Article L. 420-2 of the French Commercial Code prohibit any abuse by one or more companies holding a dominant position.

European Law

[259] Article 102 of the FEU Treaty prohibits the abuse of a dominant position within the Common Market or in a substantial part of it, provided that trade between Member States is affected.

[260] Dominance is defined as a position of economic strength enjoyed by an undertaking which enables it to prevent effective competition and to behave independently of its competitors, customers and consumers to an appreciable extent. Market shares of 50% or more are considered as strong prima facie evidence of a dominant position and those of less than 25% are generally seen as a clear indication that a company is not dominant.

[261] Article 102 does not define the concept of abuse of a dominant position in general but only lists examples of abusive behaviour:

- directly or indirectly imposing unfair purchase or selling prices or other unfair trading conditions;
- limiting production, markets or technical developments to the prejudice of consumers;
- applying discriminatory conditions to equivalent transactions with other trading parties, thereby placing them at a competitive disadvantage; or
- making the conclusion of contracts subject to acceptance by the other parties of supplementary obligations which, by their nature or according to commercial usage, have no connection with the subject of such contracts.

[262] To enforce Article 102, the Commission can issue requests for information, conduct interviews with employees, and carry out inspections of the premises of undertakings and, under narrow conditions, of the private homes of the staff of the undertakings concerned.

[263] Where the Commission considers that an undertaking has abused its dominant position; it may impose a fine of up to 10% of the undertaking's group turnover in the preceding business year. The Commission can also order the dominant undertaking to bring the infringement to an end. EU competition law is silent on the consequences of infringement of Article 102 on the validity of contracts. Member States' civil law may however fill this gap.

French Law

[264] Under French law, the definition of the abuse of dominant position is similar to the European law definition. The Competition Authority, on the one hand, and French courts, on the other hand, have jurisdiction over abuse of dominant position.

[265] The Competition Authority can order the dominant undertaking to cease its abusive practice and/or oblige it to implement any remedy (e.g., provide access to competitors). It may also impose a fine of up to 10% of the undertaking's group turnover in the preceding business year (EUR3 million for individuals), in the case the provisions of the Article L.464-2 of the French Commercial Code are characterized. The Council's decisions are subject to appeal before the Paris Court of Appeal, whose decisions may be challenged before the Supreme Court.

Rules Relating To Restrictive Practices

[266] These rules are specific to French law and mainly govern the commercial relationship between commercial companies (in particular suppliers/producers/ producers/trade). They apply to joint venture agreements or shareholders agreements too.

[267] Article L. 442-6 of the French Commercial Code prohibits the following restrictive practices:

- applying to an economic partner, or obtaining from an economic partner, discriminatory prices, terms of payment or terms and conditions of sale or purchase which are not justified by any real quid pro quo, thus creating, for that trading partner, a competitive disadvantage or advantage;
- obtaining, or seeking to obtain, from a trading partner any advantage unrelated to a commercial service effectively rendered or which is manifestly disproportionate to the value of the service rendered; taking unfair advantage of a trading partner's dependence on him or of his own purchasing power or selling capacity by subjecting him to unjustified trading conditions or obligations;
- obtaining, or seeking to obtain, an advantage as a pre-condition for the placing of orders without providing a written undertaking concerning a proportionate volume of purchases and, if appropriate, a service requested by the supplier which is the subject of a written agreement;
- obtaining, or seeking to obtain prices, terms of payment, selling arrangements or commercial cooperation conditions which are manifestly different from the general conditions of sale under the threat of a sudden total or partial severing of business relations;
- suddenly breaking off an established business relationship, even partially, without prior written notice commensurate with the duration of the business relationship and consistent with the minimum notice period determined by the multi-sector agreements in line with standard commercial practices;
- direct or indirect involvement in violation of the prohibition on reselling outside the network imposed on a distributor by a selective or exclusive distribution agreement exempted by virtue of the relevant rules of the law on competition;
- subjecting a trading partner to terms of payment which are manifestly unfair in the light of good commercial practice, and deviating, with no good reason, from the time limit indicated in the second paragraph of Article L. 441-6.

[268] An action may be brought before the competent Civil or Commercial court by any person who has an interest, by the Public Prosecutor, by the Ministry of Economy, or by the President of the Competition Authority (*Conseil de la Concurrence*). In case of such an action, the court may pronounce the following sanctions: the cessation of the practice, the nullity of the unlawful clauses or contracts declared in respect of such a practice, the reimbursement of the sums improperly paid, a fine (the amount of which shall not exceed EUR2 million) and damages for the prejudice suffered.

Regulated Activities

[269] In addition to the above rules which are applicable to all investments, a specific regulation may also be applied to companies which are active in certain areas of activities. Prior authorization or declaration to a public agency may be required or specific requirements or limitations for the investors can be set by the specific regulation.

- Such activities include banking, insurance, mining, newspapers, transport, telecommunications and medias, and military equipment. For instance, the *Autorité de Contrôle Prudentiel* (ACP) (now called *Autorité de Contrôle Prudentiel et de Résolution, or 'ACPR',* since Law n° 2013-672 of 26 July 2013) supervises credit institutions and investment firms and has disciplinary and administrative power over them. It operates with the support of the Banque de France, and has the power to grant and withdraw approval of credit institutions, investment companies and custodians (*teneurs de compte conservateur*) authorized to operate in France as well as address European passport notification to the relevant foreign regulatory authority.
- Since Law n° 2013-672 of 26 July 2013, the APCR, together with the French stock exchange market regulator, the 'AMF', where granted specific resolution powers to control and forbid the commercialization of financial products deemed as 'toxic', and/or to impose certain measures to a regulated entity in the event of evidenced financial difficulties (reorganization plan, forbidding to distribute dividends, replacement of the managers ...)

MERGER AND ACQUISITION TECHNIQUES

General Overview

Asset Acquisition versus Share Purchase

[270] Control over assets held by a French company can be secured by means of either a direct purchase of the assets or an acquisition of the shares of the company owning these assets. Two options are available within each alternative: assets or shares can be purchased for cash (acquisition) or exchanged for shares issued by the purchasing company (merger, spin off or contribution in kind: *fusion*, *scission* or *apport partiel d'actif*). Share transactions can also give rise to cash or share consideration. Another essential distinction can be made between transactions in shares of companies listed on the stock exchange and those relating to shares of unlisted companies. Variations on the above techniques which do not significantly alter applicable rules have not been dealt with in the following developments (e.g., where a company contributes part of its assets to another in return for shares but does not use the *apport partiel d'actif* procedure set out below).

[271] Please note that pursuant to French Law, only a notary (*Notaire*) can carry out a sale of real estate; the assistance of the notaire to draft the deed of transfer is not required for a transfer of shares including for shares of companies whose assets are predominantly composed of real estate assets.

Joint Venture Agreements

[272] Similarly joint ventures will not be examined in detail in the following pages because although they are a means of securing a certain degree of control over a company they do not fall strictly within the definition of mergers and acquisitions. Joint ventures in France are usually implemented by the creation of a joint company owned by the parties to the joint venture. Especially when the joint venture has a commercial activity, the *société par actions simplifiée* is the corporate form which allows the most flexibility to parties to the joint venture in organizing in the articles of association the desired decision-making process. However, parties may decide to set out rules governing their relationships in a shareholders' agreement, in particular for confidentiality reasons: the articles of association are filed with the clerk of the Commercial court in the jurisdiction in which the registered office of the company is located and anybody can obtain a copy of articles of association of French companies from the data bank of the clerks of French Commercial courts.

[273] Shareholders agreements: Shareholders agreements may be entered into by all or only some of the partners or shareholders of any kind of French company. Since they are agreements, they are not binding on the partners or shareholders who are not signatories nor on the company itself unless it has signed the shareholders' agreement. The remedy for breach of the shareholders' agreement is damages to be paid by the party in breach and seldom a specific performance. Most of the time, the shareholders agreement provide for :

(1) The company's decision-making process: appointment or dismissal of the management, organization of powers within the company or within the company's management (subject to applicable law), special rights of information for shareholders, commitment as to the vote on certain listed decisions. It should be noted that although the law does not explicitly prohibit such agreements, according to current case law, agreements whereby a shareholder, or a member of the Board of Directors, is committed in advance to vote in a specific manner are unenforceable against third parties – including the company itself when the shareholder is totally

deprived of his or her voting rights. The underlying principle here is the free exercise by each shareholder of his or her voting rights. However, a voting agreement concluded for a limited period of time which is not against the company's interests and the sole purpose of which is not the payment of compensation is enforceable against the parties to the agreement.

(2) Clauses relating to the company's shareholding: prior authorization, or pre-emptive rights, first refusal rights or first offer rights in case of transfer of shares (*clause d'agrément, droit de* préemption or *droit de premier refus* or *droit de première offre*) while a sale of shares in breach of such a clause in the articles of association would be void, a sale of shares in breach of such a clause provided for in shareholders' agreements may give right to damages except when the *mala fide* (bad faith) of the transferee can be established.

Carrying (*Portage*)

[274] An alternative method of structuring joint ventures involves the use of a *portage* contract. This is an arrangement whereby a third party (usually a bank) holds a small percentage of the shares, such percentage however being sufficient to give control to one of the other parties when added to that other party's shareholding. The third party shareholder is usually granted a put option, on a confidential basis, by the shareholder with whom the arrangement has been made and undertakes contractually to that shareholder to use his votes at shareholders' meetings in the manner indicated by the shareholder. The price of the put option is normally equal to the value of the shares plus a negotiated commission representing the consideration for the services thus rendered. The difficulty with such an arrangement is that the validity of the put option can sometimes be challenged if the purchaser is committed to acquire at a fixed price. The rationale here is that when the beneficiary of the put option can sell his shares at a fixed price, this is a means of protecting the beneficiary against the effects of corporate losses. There is a further difficulty that the voting commitment may be unenforceable, since a breach of a voting commitment can generally only give rise to monetary remedies.

[275] Such clauses (*clauses léonines*) allegedly violate the provisions of Article 1844–1 of the Civil Code. In spite of this, there is currently a tendency with French Commercial courts to recognize the validity of the carrying as such, provided such clauses are not incorporated into the articles of association of the company.

Fiducie

[276] The recent introduction of a type of trust mechanism called *fiducie* into French law would probably decrease the significance of the carrying. France signed but never ratified the Hague Convention regarding the applicable law on trusts and despite several bills proposed in the past to the French Parliament, no trust structure has been introduced in French law both for tax reasons and due to civil principle until Law 2007-211 of 19 February 2007 has been enacted.

[277] According to new Articles 2011 to 2030 of the French Civil Code as restated by Law 2007-211 of 19 February 2007 and the Modernization of the Economy Act dated 4 August 2008 and *ordonnance* n°2009-112 of 30 January 2009, *fiducie* is a transaction by which one or several settlors (*constituants*) transfer property, rights or security interests or a collection of property, rights or security interests, whether present or future, to one or several fiduciaries (*fiduciaires*) who, maintaining them separately from their own estate, act for the benefit of one or several beneficiaries (*beneficiaires*) and with a specific purpose. French law limits purposes for which a *fiducie* can validly be setup: (i) to manage an estate in the interest of the settlor (*fiducie gestion*), or (ii) to setup a security interest to the benefit of the settlor's creditor(s). *Fiducies* with gratuitous purposes are prohibited.

[278] Like for the common law trust, property, rights or security interests transferred to the *fiducie* shall constitute a special purpose estate (*patrimoine d'affectation*) protected from claims from the settlor's and the fiduciaries' creditors, save in the event of fraud.

[279] The fiduciary agreement (*contrat de fiducie*) fixes the property, rights or security interests which are transferred, the duration of the transfer, the mission and the scope of the powers of the fiduciary, and more generally the terms and conditions of the relationship between the parties, within the following limits set by the Civil Code:

- the settlor (*constituant*) can be a legal entity subject to the corporate income tax regime (Article 2015 of the Civil Code) or, since the Modernization of the Economy Act dated 4 August 2008, an individual;
- the fiduciary (*fiduciaire*) must be a bank or an investment firm regulated by the French Monetary and Financial Code or an insurance company or since the Modernization of the Economy Act dated 4 August 2008, an *avocat* (i.e., a lawyer admitted at a French Bar) (Article 2015 of the Civil Code); this is to guarantee to the settlor solvency of the fiduciary and of the transparency of the management of the property or of the rights;
- the beneficiary (*bénéficiaire*) can be either a natural person or a legal entity. The settler or the fiduciary can be the beneficiary of the fiduciary agreement;
- the transfer of the property, rights or securities provided for in the fiduciary contract is for a limited period of time which cannot exceed thirty-three years until April 1, 2009 and then ninety-nine years, as from the execution of the contract.

[280] Furthermore, pursuant to Law 2007-211 of 19 February 2007 (Article 13), the settlors and the fiduciary must be resident of a State of the European Community or of a State or territory that has concluded a tax treaty for the purposes of eliminating double taxation and which contains a clause on administrative assistance for the purposes of fighting against fraud and tax evasion with France may be a settlor of a *fiducie*.

[281] The fiduciary contract and its amendments must be registered with the tax authorities within one month from the date of its signature subject to nullity

(Article 2019 of the Civil Code); furthermore, a form of declaration of fiduciary must be filed with the tax authorities within fifteen days.

[282] Finally, decree no 2010-219 of 2 mars 2010 (Article 2020 of the Civil Code) organizes a national registry of *fiducies*.

Asset Acquisitions

Transfer of Assets for Cash versus Transfer of Assets for Shares

[283] Two types of transfer are available: the transfer of assets for cash and the transfer of assets for shares.

[284] The first category is classified as a sale which is governed by the French general law of sales (Articles 1582–1701 of the Civil Code) as well as the law of commercial acts (sale of a *fonds de commerce*). However, French law makes a distinction between the mere sale by a company of one of its assets (a sale of an isolated asset) and the sale of all of its assets, which implies the transfer of a whole business to the purchaser. And in some cases, the transfer of certain isolated assets may be considered as the transfer of a business. As soon as a transfer of all or part of the company's business (a going concern transfer or *cession de fonds de commerce*) is involved, a specific regulation is applicable in addition to the general law of sales. The most common criterion to determine if there is or is not a transfer of a business is to verify whether the transfer of assets entails a transfer of customers.

[285] The second category of asset transfers covers merger transactions (*fusions, scissions* and *apports partiels d'actif*) and generally involves the transfer of all of a company's assets or a substantial part of a company's assets to one or to several others, with the attendant consequence of the disappearance, or a 'spin off', of the 'selling' or 'contributing' company. Mergers and spin offs are regulated by a specific section of French company law.

[286] Apart from commercial or strategic considerations, the choice between these two types of transfer is largely governed by the tax and legal implications of each. This aspect will be dealt with in greater detail below Suffice it to say here that the sale of a *fonds de commerce* entails transfer taxes at a rate ranging from 0% to 5% of the value of the assets (both tangible and intangible) transferred (0% for the portion of the value ranging from EUR0 to EUR23,000, 3% for the portion ranging from EUR23,000 to EUR200,000 and 5% for the portion over EUR200,000), as well as immediate taxation of capital gains. However, mergers, in most cases, do not give rise to such a high tax burden. In spite of this substantial drawback, a sale of the *fonds de commerce* is usually used where a seller either runs his or her business individually, without incorporating a company, or prefers to receive payment in cash, and/or does not wish to remain involved in any way, whether as a shareholder or as a guarantor, with the business he or she has transferred. In fact, the purchaser of a *fonds de commerce* in principle acquires only assets and the seller is thus not requested to deliver warranty and indemnity provisions in favour of the purchaser as in the case of share acquisitions.

Sale of Assets

Sale of Fonds de Commerce

The *Fonds de Commerce* Purchase Agreement

[287] Although it is often loosely equated with a 'business', a *fonds de commerce* is strictly a collection of assets, tangible and intangible, which enables a person or company to operate a business of a commercial or industrial nature. It has a legal existence which is distinct from that of its constituent parts, and is classified as moveable property which may, as such, be sold, leased or charged in its own right.

[288] There is no definition of the *fonds de commerce* in the Commercial Code. In practice, the courts have narrowed down its composition to the existence of a *clientèle* (customers) which is the core asset of the *fonds de commerce*. In addition to this intangible asset, the parties can agree to include other assets related to the *clientèle*, e.g., certain tangible assets (machines, furniture and equipment, fixtures and fittings, inventories) and certain intangible assets (trade names, leases and intellectual property rights). It will at once be obvious that the *fonds de commerce*, as French law understands it, does not include per se a title to real property (*immeubles*), receivables or contractual rights. These must accordingly be specifically mentioned in the contract of sale if they are to be included in the transfer as well as the inventory, which is subject to a specific tax regime. Real property conveyance may only be perfected by means of a separate notarial deed; however, the lease of the premises where the business is operated is a substantial item of the *fonds de commerce*, and an assignment of the lease agreement can be considered as a transfer of *fonds de commerce*.

[289] A contract of sale must be drawn up which must contain certain information required by law, such as the name of the previous seller (if any), the date and type of the contract of sale, the purchase price (with a breakdown of the price between the tangible items and the intangible items), a list of the existing charges or liens (if any), the turnover for the preceding three years or number of years of possession if less than three years, the operating result during the same period of time, the date and duration of the lease (if any) and the name and address of the landlord or assignor where applicable (Article L.141-1 of the Commercial Code amended by act n° 2012-387 of March 22, 2012).

[290] Failure to include any of the above information renders the contract of sale voidable at the sole option of the purchaser. Incorrect information exposes the seller to repayment of the full purchase price in exchange for the transfer of the *fonds de commerce* back to the original owner provided that the purchaser brings an action before the courts within one year of the effective date of the sale.

[291] The provisions referred to above apply to any document, irrespective of its form or avowed purpose, which permits or implements the transfer of a *fonds de commerce*. They are applicable in particular to reciprocal put and call options relating to a *fonds de commerce* (*promesse synallagmatique*) and to certain call options (*promesse unilatérale de vente*) providing for a substantial cancellation fee. They are also applicable to sales subject to a condition precedent.

[292] In practice the execution of the contract of sale is frequently preceded by another (usually shorter) document (e.g., *protocole d'accord*, memorandum of understanding, *promesse de vente* combined with a purchase option) which, depending on the precise terms of this pre-contract, may contain a *promesse synallagmatique de vente et d'achat* (where both parties are committed) or a *promesse unilatérale de vente* (where the seller alone is committed). In the latter case it should be noted that the commitment is void if the document is not registered with the local tax office within ten days following the date of execution of the document A fixed registration tax is payable at this stage (currently EUR125).

[293] The sale of a *fonds de commerce*, in addition to specific legislation regulating particular aspects of such transactions, is subject to the general French law of sales (Articles 1582–1701 of the Civil Code), which contains a number of provisions relating to guarantees (Articles 1625–1649 of the Civil Code). These include a guarantee of title (*garantie d'éviction*) and a guarantee against latent defects (*garantie des vices cachés*). The latter provision gives rise in practice to the greatest number of claims and French law, together with the case law relating to it, will be briefly summarized before its application to a *fonds de commerce* is considered.

[294] A latent defect is one which is not readily apparent to an ordinary layman (although, under certain circumstances, the courts will take into account the professional and technical capacity of the purchaser in order to assess whether, in light of the nature of the latent defect, a professional purchaser should have detected it) at the time of the sale and which, when revealed subsequently, seriously impedes the normal use of the object sold. The manifestation of a latent defect entitles the purchaser, at his sole option, either to a reduction of the purchase price a posteriori or to a rescission of the sale. The courts have discretion in their assessment of the existence of a latent defect and as to the extent of the loss suffered by the purchaser. Action must be brought within two years from the date of discovery of the defect, failing which the action is rejected or becomes time-barred by the statute of limitations. It is lawful to provide contractually for a more restricted or more extensive guarantee, although restrictive clauses are valid only where they occur in a contract between parties who are professionals in the same field or specialization.

[295] Application of the latent defect concept to a *fonds de commerce* raises many difficulties. It has also resulted in abundant case law arising from the fact that the courts have a wide degree of discretion in this regard. The principle is that latent defects are assessed not in relation to the *fonds de commerce* as a whole but in relation to each of the assets which form its constituent parts. Accordingly, while certain circumstances are clear instances of the existence of a 'latent defect' (e.g., an infringing trademark or a voidable patent), in the majority of cases the availability of legal protection is uncertain, and in any event dependent on the outcome of time-consuming court proceedings.

[296] In practice the parties rely on contractually agreed representations and warranties which, although they do not remove altogether the need for court resolution of disputes, at least tend to confine the issue to one of interpretation of a clause. The practice of warranty clauses is not as widespread in France as it is elsewhere because of the continental preference for brevity in drafting and the greater reliance placed on judicial solutions. However, increasing exposure to cross-border deals has brought about wider acceptance of such internationally used drafting standards and methods. Nevertheless, these are not always appropriate for the transfer of a *fonds de commerce*, where the purchaser only acquires certain assets and where liabilities are in principle excluded unless agreed otherwise between the parties.

[297] Contractual rights and obligations are not included in the French concept of *fonds de commerce* and are therefore not transferred when a *fonds de commerce* is sold. There are only three exceptions to this rule provided by specific legislation: contracts of employment (Article L.1224–1 of the Labour Code), insurance contracts (Article L.121–10 of the Insurance Code) and publishing contracts (Articles L.111-1 et seq. and L.132-16 of the Intellectual Property Code). The landlord cannot refuse the assignment to the purchaser of the *fonds de commerce* of the leases relating to premises where the business (*fonds de commerce*) is carried out.

[298] Other types of contract cannot be transferred unless they are specifically listed in the contract of sale. This rule applies *inter alia* to equipment and financial leases, loans and guarantees, distribution and agency contracts, franchises and contracts for the sale or supply of goods.

[299] While transfer as between seller and purchaser is perfected by the execution of the contract of sale, the transfer is not valid and enforceable against the other contracting parties and third parties in general (e.g., creditors) unless the consent of such other contracting parties has been obtained (usually by letter). Legal authors (and many legal practitioners) tend to consider that mere notification by letter to the other contracting parties should be sufficient, but this view is not founded on any law or court decision.

[300] As regards receivables, consent of the seller's debtor is not required for the transfer to be valid. However the transfer is not valid as against the debtor and third parties until notice thereof has been formally served on the debtor by a process-server (*huissier*) (Article 1690 of the Civil Code).

Undisclosed Liabilities and Protection of Creditors

[301] In order to inform creditors of the seller (who may or may not have a charge or lien over the *fonds de commerce*) that the *fonds de commerce* has been sold, French law provides that the sale must be published within fifteen days in a local legal gazette, and in a centralized legal publication, the *Bulletin Officiel des Annonces Civiles et Commerciales* (Articles L.141-12 (amended by act n°2012-387 of 22 March 2012) to L.141-17 and R.123-212 of the Commercial Code). If creditors make themselves known to the seller (or his designated agent) within the following ten days, they are entitled to be paid immediately out of the proceeds of sale, provided the seller recognizes the debt (or a court declares the amount to be due, in case of dispute). In this connection the purchase price is almost always deposited with an escrow agent, who is then responsible for the receipt of creditors' declarations and for payment of amounts due. In any event the purchase price must not be paid to the seller before the necessary publications have been made, and the appropriate time periods have expired. Otherwise the purchaser is liable to the seller's creditors up to the full amount of the purchase price.

[302] If the price is not sufficient to pay off all creditors, any creditor may, within twenty days of the last published announcement in the *Bulletin Officiel des Annonces Civiles et Commerciales,* make a formal offer to purchase the *fonds de commerce* at a price which must be higher by at least one sixth than the price to be paid by the contemplated purchaser. A public auction is then held at which the *fonds de commerce* is sold.

Location Gérance of a Fonds de commerce

[303] The *location gérance* agreement is a specific lease agreement regulated by Articles L.144-1 to L.144-13. and R.144-1 and seq. of the Commercial Code, whereby the owner of a *fonds de commerce* leases it to a third party who carries on the business at his own risk and expense. The lessor remains the owner of the assets constituting the *fonds de commerce* (tangible and intangible assets). Receivables and payables remain in the name of the lessor.

[304] The two following conditions must be met prior to entering into a *location gérance* agreement:

- as the 'location gérance' is a commercial act, the lessee qualifies for the title of merchant. As a consequence, he must register with the trade and companies registry within fifteen days from the beginning of his commercial activity; and
- the business *fonds de commerce* to be leased must have been operated personally by the lessor for a minimum period of two years.

[305] However, these two conditions or only one of them can be waived by virtue of a special court decision at the request of the lessor, after the court has obtained the advice of the Public Prosecutor on such a waiver.

[306] Subject to the precise terms of the *location-gérance* agreement, the lessor transfers the responsibilities of running the business to the lessee who assumes the risk of incurring losses, or the opportunity of making profits. In exchange for the right to run the business, the lessee pays the lessor an appropriate royalty which can be either fixed or proportional to the turnover. The lessor's charges will mainly consist of depreciation.

[307] Insofar as the arrangement is at 'arm's length', the royalty is deductible for tax purposes by the lessee and is considered as a profit to the lessor.

[308] The agreement must be concluded for a fixed period which is renewable and the agreement must be published in a legal gazette within the fifteen days following its execution. The parties are free to determine their respective rights and obligations as well as the terms and conditions on which the agreement may be terminated. The lessor must continue to pay the lease rentals related to the premises where the business is operated, since this type of lease is not transferred under the *location gérance.*

[309] During the six months following the announcement in a legal gazette, the lessor is jointly and severally liable with the lessee for the debts the latter has incurred in operating the *fonds de commerce*. Furthermore, the lessor remains jointly liable with the lessee during the whole term of the *location gérance* for the payment of all corporate taxes incurred in operating the business.

[310] Unless otherwise provided by the *location gérance* agreement, the lessee is free to decide whether to continue or discontinue the agreements related to the *fonds de commerce*, such as distribution agreements and insurance agreements. However employment contracts must be taken over in accordance with Article L.1224–1 of the Labour Code. Inventories are generally sold by the lessor to the lessee simultaneously with execution of the *location gérance* agreement.

[311] The *location gérance* of a *fonds de commerce* may be used as a test period to enable potential investors to get accustomed to the business prior to purchasing it.

[312] In cases of deadlock between the investors, or if one of the investors wishes to withdraw, the *location gérance* agreement can easily be terminated provided there is a clause providing for termination. Publication formalities are required with the Trade and Companies Registry and in a legal gazette upon the expiration of the agreement.

[313] From a tax viewpoint, the *location gérance* method is neutral and does not involve any immediate taxation as it is not considered as a cessation of business. It should nevertheless only be considered as a temporary solution since it is related to a transfer of the running of a *fonds de commerce* and not to a transfer of the business itself.

Merger Transactions

[314] Under French company law, there are three types of merger transaction: *fusion*, *scission* and *apport partiel d'actif*. A *fusion* is either a *fusion-absorption* where a company completely absorbs another company (merger by amalgamation) or a *fusion-création* where two companies merge to form a new company (merger by consolidation). In both cases the shareholders of the absorbed company receive shares of the absorbing company. A *scission* is a transaction by which all the assets and liabilities of a company are contributed to newly created companies. The shareholders of the contributing company receive shares of all the receiving companies. An *apport partiel d'actif* (or spin-off) is a transfer of part of the assets, with or without liabilities, of a company to another company in exchange for shares of the receiving company. The rules applicable to the *apport partiel d'actif* will be reviewed below.

'Fusion' and 'Scission'

[315] The *fusion* and the *scission* are governed by the rules contained in Article 1844-4 of the Civil Code and Articles L.236-1 to L.236-32 and R.236-1 to R.236-20 of the Commercial Code. For this reason, references to *fusion* in this section must always be regarded as including *scission*, although the *scission* is infrequent in France

because of an unfavourable tax regime for such transactions because of the difficulty in satisfying all the conditions of the favourable tax regime (as described below).

General Characteristics of a *Fusion*

[316] A *fusion* entails the transfer of all the assets and liabilities of the absorbed company to and for the benefit of the absorbing company. The absorbing company will have title to all the assets of the acquired company and will also assume all its liabilities.

[317] Since all its assets and liabilities are transferred, the acquired company is automatically wound up. The shareholders of the absorbed company will receive shares of the absorbing company issued by way of an increase of the latter's share capital, the amount of such increase to be no higher than the net asset value of the absorbed company. The absorbing company may also offer cash provided the amount offered does not exceed 10% of the total value of the shares issued.

[318] Non-compliance with this rule will entail disqualification of the transaction as a *fusion* and its treatment as a sale of assets.

[319] If the absorbing company owns shares in the absorbed company, it cannot receive its own shares in exchange and must accordingly limit the increase of its share capital by an amount sufficient to permit the issue of new shares to all shareholders of the absorbed company other than itself. Similarly, if the absorbed company owns some of its own shares, no shares of the absorbing company may be issued in exchange for these shares. When the absorbing company owns 100% of the absorbed company' shares, the decree of 9 November 2011 provides the draft of merger should not list (i) the terms of transfer of the shares or stocks, (ii) the date from which these shares or stocks give entitlement to profit, (iii) the amount of the *soulte* (cash payment) or the *prime de fusion* (premium).

[320] Pursuant to law n°2012-387 dated 22 March 2012, a Company selling part of its assets (*apport partiel d'actifs*) may decide with the buyer to realize the operation according to provisions of Articles L.236-1 to L.236-6 of the French Commercial Code.

Valuation of the Companies

[321] Valuation of both the absorbing company and the absorbed company is the first step in the implementation of a merger. Due diligence is generally carried out by a firm of auditors or accountants. Various methods of valuation are available to determine the 'fair market' value of the companies. The *Autorité des Marchés Financiers* ('AMF') (formerly *Commission des Opérations de Bourse*, or 'COB') recommends that several assessments should be made using different methods, the final value being established by way of comparison. To valuate the assets to be contributed, the book value must be used when the merger is contemplated between companies which are controlled by the same company and when this control is not altered by the merger. The book value cannot be used to value the companies to determine the exchange ratio, including within the same group. The exchange ratio must always be fixed based on market value.

[322] Where the value of the shares of the absorbing company exceeds their par value, a premium will be created and entered into a special account (*prime de fusion*) on its balance sheet. The shareholders, acting upon the proposal of the management of the company, may decide to use this account either to pay for expenses incurred by the company in connection with the transaction or to charge it to a reserve account.

Draft Merger Agreement or *Projet de Fusion*

[323] The management (Board of Directors in a *société anonyme*, *gérant* in a *société à' responsabilité limitée* and *président* in a *société par actions simplifiée*) of each of the companies involved are jointly responsible for preparing a draft merger agreement, which must as a matter of law contain the following mandatory information: the form, name and registered office of all the companies involved in the *fusion*; the purpose, aims and conditions of the *fusion*; the dates on which the companies will close their accounts for the purpose of fixing the terms and conditions of the transaction; the effective date of the *fusion* for accounting purposes (the *fusion* is usually implemented with retroactive effect to the closing dates referred to above); a description of the assets and liabilities transferred and their value; the exchange ratio used for the transfers of the shares concerned and the amount of the premium; the date of transfer of the shares and the date as from which the shares have a right to the profits in the company. The draft merger agreement must be approved by the management of each company and signed by the chief executive officer (*Président-Directeur Général* or *Directeur Général* in a *société anonyme*, *gérant* in a *société à responsabilité limitée* and *Président* in a *société par actions simplifiée*) of each of them. Prior consultation with the *comité d'entreprise* must take place before the execution of the draft merger agreement, and before the Board of Directors' meeting approving such execution.

[324] The agreement is then filed with clerk of the Commercial court and a summary of the mandatory information which it contains must be published in a legal gazette. When one or both of the companies is a public company, a notice must also be published in a special bulletin (BALO). These formalities must be complied with at the latest one month before the date of the extraordinary general meetings of shareholders convened to vote on the transaction.

Official Valuation and Shareholders' Approval

[325] A *commissaire à la fusion* (merger controller), appointed by the President of the Commercial Court at the request of either party or jointly by all the companies involved, must draft two reports:

- a report on the specific terms of the merger within which the merger controller checks that the value per share of the respective companies is appropriate and that the exchange ratio is fair. Such report will also indicate the method of valuation used, the validity of this method, the resulting values and any specific problems encountered; and

- a report on the valuation of the contributions in kind and confirming that the net assets contributed are at least equal to the amount of the share capital increase to be approved by the shareholders as a result of such contribution. Such reports must be made available to the shareholders of all the companies involved at the registered office of each company at least one month prior to the date of the extraordinary shareholders' meetings of both companies; the second report must be filed with the clerk of the Commercial court at least one month prior to the date of the extraordinary shareholders' meetings. In the event of fusion of the French 'Société par actions' (SA, SCA, SAS), specific provisions must be observed.

The appointment of a *commissaire à la fusion* is not necessary if the absorbing company holds 100% or 90% of its subsidiary.

[326] The management of each company must also draft a report which must be made available to the shareholders prior to the extraordinary shareholders' meeting called to vote on the *fusion*. In addition to providing information similar to that contained in the report of the *commissaire à la fusion*, the management's report must indicate the economic and legal reasons for the *fusion*.

[327] Shareholders of both the absorbing and the absorbed company will vote on the merger itself and on its terms and conditions as described in the draft merger agreement (*traité de fusion*), and the shareholders' meeting may amend the draft merger agreement. Such resolutions are passed by the qualified majority required by law and by the articles of association for an extraordinary meeting (to amend the articles of association), except for a merger with a *société par actions simplifiée* as an absorbing company which may require an unanimous vote of the shareholders of the absorbed company.

[328] The act n°2011-525 of 17 May 2011 simplifies the rules governing mergers and divisions of companies. If the absorbing company holds 100% of the shares of the subsidiary absorbed, the draft merger agreement should not list the share exchange ratio, the amount of the cash payment, the terms relating to the allotment of shares in the absorbing company, and the date from which these shares or stocks give entitlement to profit. The approval of the general meeting of both companies of the merger is not required if (i) the draft merger agreement has been published one month before the merger, (ii) all the shareholders of the absorbing company can consult documents (draft merger agreement, annual accounts, management reports of the last three years, and were appropriated, accounting statement) at the registered office one month before the merger.

If the absorbing company holds more than 90% of the shares of the subsidiary absorbed, the approval of the merger by the absorbing company is not required if (i) the draft merger agreement has been published one month before the general meeting of the absorbing company to approve the merger, (ii) the shareholders can consult documents (draft merger agreement, annual accounts, management reports of the last three years, and were appropriated, accounting statement, reports by the company's administrative or management body, and expert reports) at the registered office one month before the merger.

[329] In both cases, no exchange of shares between the shares of the absorbed company and of the absorbing company takes place nor any share capital increase at the level of the absorbing company.

[330] It should be added that where one of the companies involved has issued different classes of shares, the *fusion* must be submitted for a prior approval to a meeting of each of the special classes of holders.

Consequences of the Merger

[331] The *fusion* will be effective on the following dates:

- in the case of creation of one or more new companies, at the date of registration with the Trade and Companies Registry of the last new company; and
- in cases where existing companies only are involved, at the date on which the last shareholders' meeting to be held has approved the *fusion*, except as otherwise provided in the merger agreement.

[332] If the *traité de fusion* provides for a different date, this date must not be later than the end of the absorbing company's current fiscal year or before the beginning of the absorbed company's current fiscal year. The retroactive effect (or the deferred effect) of the merger or spin-off is only possible in cases where the absorbing company is already an existing company.

As a result of the transfer of liabilities entailed by the *fusion*, the absorbing company becomes, by operation of law, the debtor of all creditors of the absorbed company in lieu of the latter. Any creditor (other than a bondholder) of the absorbed or of the absorbing company whose claim is prior to the date of publication of the planned merger in a legal gazette may oppose the *fusion* by an action in the Commercial Court within thirty days of such publication. This opposition cannot in fact prevent the continuation of the *fusion* from going forward. The Commercial Court may reject the opposition. Alternatively it may order the absorbed company to repay these debts or to provide security if the absorbing company so offers and if the security is accepted as sufficient. Failing repayment of the debts or the offer of security as ordered, the *fusion* will not be enforceable against the creditor, who will benefit from a preferential right compared to the creditors of the absorbing company in respect of the transferred assets.

[333] Where the absorbed company has issued bonds, other than bonds exchangeable for shares, it may decide either to submit the planned merger to a bondholders' meeting or to repay the bonds. In the first case, the bondholders may reject the merger, although such refusal cannot stop the merger from going forward.

[334] When the bondholders have been consulted but have refused the proposed merger, the Board of Directors' of the absorbed company may decide to bypass the refusal of the bondholders, which decision must be published in a legal gazette (and in a special bulletin (BALO) if the company is a public company). In such a case the representatives of the bondholders may within a thirty-day period as from the publication oppose the merger before the Commercial Court. The Commercial Court may either reject such opposition or order the reimbursement of the bonds or the provision of security if the absorbing company so offers and if the security is considered as sufficient.

[335] In the absence of reimbursement of the bonds ordered by the Commercial Court, the bondholders will become bondholders in the absorbing company which will have to assume the liabilities of the absorbed company with respect to this bond issue.

[336] When the absorbed company has issued bonds with attached warrants or bonds convertible into shares, the same rules discussed above apply, although in the case of bonds convertible into shares the merger is subject to the prior approval of the general meeting of such holders of bonds convertible into shares and the company does not have the option to repay the bonds instead of consulting the bondholders. In the event the holders of bonds convertible into shares reject the proposed merger, such a refusal cannot stop the merger transaction and the above-mentioned rules governing opposition will apply.

[337] When the absorbed company has issued bonds exchangeable for shares, the merger is subject to the prior approval of the general meeting of such bondholders. The merger transaction shall not occur in the absence of approval of such bondholders on the merger.

Apport Partiel d'Actif (Spin-off)

[338] An *apport partiel d'actif* is a scheme by which a company transfers part of its business to another company, the consideration being shares issued by the receiving company. The contributing company may either transfer one or more of its assets (such as premises or an interest in another company) or a set of assets capable of being organized as an independent business (such as a division of a company). According to the act of 22 March 2012 and the new Article L.236-6-1 of the French Commercial Code, the *apport partiel d'actif* may be regarded as a *fusion* or a *scission* whatever the legal form of the company making the transaction. The AMF strongly recommends the adoption of these rules where the contributing company is a listed company which transfers a significant part of its assets. Where the assets transferred can be regarded as an independent business, the special tax treatment provided for *fusions* and *scissions* is available.

[339] The procedure for the *apport partiel d'actif* is as follows. First, the management of each of the companies involved draft an *apport partiel d'actif* agreement which must indicate each asset and each liability transferred together with their valuation and which usually contains representations and warranties provided by the contributing company. A *commissaire aux apports* (official valuer) must then be appointed by the Commercial Court at the request of the management of both companies. The *commissaire aux apports* will draft a report containing his or her valuation of the assets contributed. This report must be filed with the Trade and

Companies Registry and made available to the shareholders of the receiving company at the registered office at least eight days prior to the date of the extraordinary shareholders' meeting. Finally the shareholders of the receiving company will be asked to vote on the *apport partiel d'actif* and to increase the capital by an amount equal to the approved contribution. The relevant resolution must be passed by a qualified majority required by law and the articles of association for the extraordinary meeting (to amend the articles of association). In an SAS, the majority rules are determined in the articles of association but cannot be lower than the simple majority of the voting rights of the shareholders present or represented.

[340] According to the act of 22 March 2012, when an *apport partiel d'actifs* is made by a absorbed company wholly owned by the absorbing one, the appointment of a *commissaire aux apports* to establish (i) the valuation of the assets contributed, (ii) the approval of the shareholders' meeting and (iii) the capital increase are not required anymore (Article L.236-6-1 of the French Commercial Code).

[341] When the partial contribution covers all the assets, liabilities, rights and obligations of a business, a contribution with retroactive effect is from a practical viewpoint almost mandatory. In fact the assets contributed, as identified and valued in the draft agreement, must still exist at the date the resolution is passed if no retroactive effect were provided for. In practice, of course, this is impossible, especially in the case of inventories.

Share Acquisitions

[342] Instead of acquiring the assets of a company by means of a sale of the *fonds de commerce* or a merger (*fusion, scission* or *apport partiel d'actif*), a potential acquirer may seek to obtain control through an acquisition of the shares of the company owning the assets. Preference for this solution may derive from the fact that share acquisitions are simpler (at least for unlisted companies) and in certain cases more effective from a tax viewpoint (this is certainly the case when compared to the sale of a *fonds de commerce*).

General Overview

Acquisition of a Company's Control

[343] While the percentage of shares acquired does not have any impact on the structure and procedure for implementing the transaction (except in the case of listed companies), it does have significant consequences with regard to control of the target company. While there are several statutory definitions of control, each of which applies to specific circumstances, control in practice means the ability to run the company without hindrance, whether at management level or by means of shareholders' resolutions.

Control in the Shareholders' Meetings

[344] In the most common types of commercial company (the SA, SAS and the SARL) management is appointed and annual accounts approved by a shareholders' resolution passed by a simple majority. The ability to command 50% of the votes either by direct ownership or through contractual arrangements with other shareholders results in the exercise of financial control by one or a group of shareholders. Furthermore, as there are various types of securities which may be issued by *sociétés par actions*, control is assessed in such companies on the voting rights (in order to take into account double voting rights, preferred shares and stock options granted to employees under stock option plans) instead of on the shares. Absolute control of a company entails the ability to pass extraordinary resolutions.

Control at the Management Level

[345] In an SA control of the Board of Directors is also necessary, since the *President Directeur Général* (president and managing director) is appointed by a board resolution passed by a simple majority. Control at the management level therefore requires that the acquirer be represented by more than half of directors on the board. In an SARL management consists of a single *gérant* who is appointed by an ordinary resolution of the shareholders. As regards the other types of company (SAS or *sociétés de personnes*), special attention should be drawn to the articles of association which in principle have flexibility to determine the organization of corporate management in terms of quorum and majority required to pass resolutions. With respect to the SCS or the SCA, control of management is a key issue, as management is in essence independent from the shareholding. These considerations should be borne in mind when the structure of the transaction is being negotiated.

Control and Related Consequences with Respect to the Acquisition

[346] In addition to the control over the management and the resolutions passed at the shareholders' meetings, the issue of whether a potential purchaser acquires control of a company or not results in significant practical effects.

Application to the Acquisition of Control of Specific Regulations Governing the Sale of a *Fonds de Commerce* (Going Concern)

[347] Pursuant to Law No. 70–9 of 2 January 1970 (as amended by Ordinance No. 2004-634 of 1 July 2004; Law No. 2006-872 of 13 July 2006 and Law No. 2006-1770 of 30 December 2006, Law n° 2009-323 of 25 March 2009, Law n° 2012-387 of 22 March 2012), governing real estate brokerage agency, any intermediary, especially any agent or broker, in charge of the sale of real estate or *fonds de commerce* must hold a professional card issued by the *Préfet* as well as a special power of attorney in order to carry out such activities. Under Article 1 of Law No. 70–9, these statutory provisions apply to any individual or entity which carries out in the ordinary course of its business intermediary transactions with respect to the purchase or sale of non-negotiable shares of a company with underlying assets including real property or a *fonds de commerce*.

[348] On the basis of Article 1, the acquisition of control of a *société de personnes* or of an SARL falls within the scope of Law No. 70–9, unlike the acquisition of control of an SA, an SAS or an SCA, as the shares of these companies are freely negotiable. Despite these clear provisions, the *Cour de Cassation* has held that the sale of the shares of a company running a *fonds de commerce*, irrespective of its corporate legal form, falls within the scope of Law No. 70–9, as the transfer of shares is necessarily related to the transfer of the underlying *fonds de commerce*. Although this decision was criticized, it follows therefrom that any company acting as an intermediary in the sale of corporate control (whether in an SARL, SA or SCA) should hold a professional card as well as a special power of attorney in order to exercise its functions.

Tax Consequences of the Acquisition of a Company's Control

[349] It should be noted that in the past the acquisition of most of the shares of a company was considered by the tax authorities as the sale of the underlying *fonds de commerce* and subject accordingly to a registration tax on the value of the assets transferred. However the *Cour de Cassation* issued significant decisions in 1984 which ruled against the doctrine of the tax administration on the basis that the transaction remains a purchase of shares and does not result in the creation of a new legal entity. Since then, the tax administration has reversed its previous rulings and has declared that it will no longer treat such transactions as the sale of a *fonds de commerce* unless the companies involved are wound up and replaced by a newly created company. The change of control of a company also does not trigger the forfeiture of its tax losses carried-forward.

Commercial Nature of the Transaction

[350] Although the purchase of shares is in principle considered to be a civil transaction, it becomes commercial if the transaction results in the purchaser acquiring control of the company concerned. Accordingly, the stock purchase agreement can validly provide for an arbitration clause and the rules governing evidence and statute of limitations in commercial transactions are more flexible (evidence may be produced by all means and statute of limitations is extended to ten years). The sellers are jointly liable, unless expressly provided otherwise, if they give representations.

Transfer of Shares of Unlisted Companies

Structure of the Transaction

[351] There are usually three stages involved in implementing a transaction. The first is the exchange of a preliminary document (memorandum of understanding, letter of intent, etc.) which contains the principal features of the transaction and which may be legally binding, depending on whether the parties have committed to buy and sell the shares respectively. The document often provides for the possibility of due diligence (financial, tax and legal) and sets a date for the final closing following the fulfilment of certain conditions precedent. These may include obtaining necessary regulatory authorizations (antitrust regulations) or shareholders' approval for the transfer of the shares (when such approval is required by the articles of association) or the confirmation, by the due diligence to be carried out, of the accuracy of the information supplied by the seller with respect to the target company.

[352] Where both parties are committed and there is no condition precedent to be fulfilled, the agreement should technically be regarded as a sale, with the consequence that registration tax on the purchase price should in principle be paid at the time.

[353] In most share acquisition transactions, the purchase price paid by the purchaser (fair market price) is far above the nominal value of the shares of the target company. Pursuant to Article 1591 of the Civil Code and pursuant to French case law, the purchase price in the contract of sale must be determined by the parties or at least determinable on the basis of the provisions of the sale agreement itself and without the necessity for a further agreement between the parties subsequent to the transfer of the shares; failure to comply with this requirement results in the sale contract being null and void.

[354] The sale agreement must therefore (a) either determine the purchase price prior to the transfer of the shares, or (b) include an objective formula on the basis of which the purchase price can be automatically determined, or alternatively (c) provide for recourse to a third party pursuant to Article 1592 of the Civil Code, which provides that *the determination of the purchase price may be left to the arbitration of a third party; if the third party is unwilling or unable to make the estimate, there is no sale.*

[355] Where the parties leave the determination to the decision of an independent expert(s) under Article 1592 of the Civil Code, the parties must either designate the expert(s) prior to the transfer of the shares (the expert(s) frequently being selected from among the professionals responsible for the financial audit of the company) or must provide in the sale agreement for the expert(s) to be appointed by a designated court where the parties cannot agree on the choice of expert(s). Failure to provide expressly as aforesaid renders the sale agreement null and void for uncertainty of the purchase price. The provisions concerning the purchase price should accordingly be drafted with care.

Documentation: Warranty Provisions

[356] Once the preliminary due diligence and the other conditions precedent have been completed a full agreement should *normally* be drawn up and signed by both parties. The greater part of this document will consist of the declarations and warranties and indemnity provisions.

Statutory Warranty Provisions

[357] Unlike the purchase of a *fonds de commerce*, a transfer of shares also results of transfer of a portion of the liabilities as well as the corporate assets of the target company. As a result the purchaser always tries as far as possible to supplement the warranty provisions of the Civil Code by contractual warranty provisions.

[358] The negotiation of adequate warranty provisions is crucial since in the absence of such clauses only the Civil Code provisions relating to guarantees (Articles 1625–1649) would apply. However protection under these articles is limited in practice, since the courts have held that the guarantee against latent defects applies only to the shares themselves and not to the assets owned by the company. Legal protection is therefore more restricted in the case of a sale of shares than in the case of a sale of a *fonds de commerce*.

[359] Another application of the statutory protection is the ability for the purchaser, on the basis of Article 1116 of the Civil Code, to seek a judgment rendering the sale of shares null and void if he or she can prove that his or her consent was vitiated because of wilful misrepresentation (*dol*). It must be borne in mind that evidence of wilful misrepresentation is admitted only on the strictest terms by French courts. An action for wilful misrepresentation will only succeed if all the following conditions are satisfied:

- the existence of positive acts or (in certain cases) omissions on the part of the seller aimed at misleading the buyer (such as the production of forged documents, lies or withholding of information);
- the existence of a clear intention to mislead the buyer;
- the buyer must have relied on the action of the seller to consent to the transaction;
- the mistake of the buyer must be legitimate taking into account the level of his or her professional expertise.

[360] If all the above conditions are met and if the buyer does not choose to render the sale null and void, he or she may instead initiate a tort action against the seller.

Contractual Warranty Provisions

[361] As a result of the case law referred to above and the limited effects of the statutory warranties, the contractual warranty provisions are drafted in great detail. Although the contractual warranty provisions are designated under the general term of *garantie de passif*, this term covers in practice various types of warranty which result in different commitments for the issuer. A broad distinction should be drawn between the following.

- The strict *garantie de passif* where the seller who guarantees under numerous declarations against certain risks arising from periods prior to completion of the sale or prior to the guaranteed balance sheet (such as accounting, financial, tax, labour law, contractual or environmental risks) and undertakes on a direct basis to indemnify the creditors of the company or the company itself.
- The price revision clause, pursuant to which the seller guarantees the net equity of the company sold at the same level as it appears in the guaranteed balance sheet. In that case, if the guarantee is called, the seller indemnifies the buyer in respect of any reduction in the net equity of the company pro

rata to his former shareholding. It is questionable whether this does not render the purchase price undetermined or undeterminable at the time of the sale agreement (for the reasons set out above). While the strict *garantie de passif* is in some ways more favourable to the purchaser, since the seller's undertaking is for an unlimited amount (unless otherwise provided), the price revision clause is to be recommended to the seller since:

(a) his or her payment undertaking may not in any case exceed the purchase price paid by the purchaser even if the liabilities prove subsequently to be higher; and

(b) being a guarantee of net equity all plusses and minuses are set off against each other.

- A full assets and liabilities guarantee where the seller guarantees, on a line-by-line basis, the assets and liabilities of the guaranteed balance sheet.

[362] It should be emphasized that facts regarding the company which may have been disclosed to the potential purchaser in the course of the audits conducted prior to the acquisition, in particular facts which may have given rise to the constitution of reserves, are often excluded from the scope of the indemnification clause.

Closing of the Transaction

[363] Closing requires the execution of a document of transfer and compliance with certain formalities designed to perfect the transfer. In addition a meeting of the shareholders or of the Board of Directors must in certain cases be held to authorize the transfer or to approve the transferee as a new shareholder or to appoint new management.

Legal Formalities (other than Tax Registration Payment)

[364] Transfer documents and formalities are not the same in the case of a transfer of shares (*actions*) of *sociétés par actions* (SA, SAS or SCA), or transfer of shares of *sociétés de personnes, sociétés civiles* or an SARL (see Chapter 1). To transfer shares of an SA, SAS or SCA, the seller will complete and sign a share transfer form (*ordre de mouvement*) which is then delivered to the purchaser, and then by the purchaser to the issuing company. Upon receipt of this document the company must record the appropriate entries into the company's shareholders registry, i.e., the shareholders individual accounts and the share transfer registry (*register des mouvements de titres*). Pursuant to Articles L.228-1 and R.228-10 of the Commercial Code, the ownership of the shares is transferred on the date the transfer is recorded in the company's shareholders registry. However the sale of the shares is perfected as between the parties on the date on which consent to the transaction is expressed: this will usually take place on the closing date (when all the conditions precedent have been fulfilled and the share transfer form is executed by the seller) although from a legal point of view the relevant transfer date may sometimes take place prior to the closing date when the parties have agreed upon the object and the price of the sale. In fact, pursuant to Article 1589 of the Civil Code, a commitment to purchase is valid and legally binding when the parties have agreed on the underlying object of the sale and on the price. Since shares are dematerialized in France since 5 November 2004, no share certificates are issued to the purchaser of the shares. However, as any shareholder, he or she may request the company to deliver a document certifying how many shares of the company are recorded on his or her shareholder's account (*attestation d'inscription en compte*).

[365] In the case of an SARL or of a *société de personnes*, the transfer of shares (*parts sociales*) which are not negotiable must comply with the cumbersome procedure described in the first section of this chapter: the transfer must be recorded in a written agreement and the sale is valid as against the company on the date on which this agreement is officially delivered at the registered office of the company against a receipt signed by the *gérant*, or on the date on which notice of the sale is officially served on the company, with a copy of the agreement, by a *huissier* (process-server). The transfer is valid as against third parties only when copies of the agreement have been officially filed with the Trade and Companies Registry.

[366] The recent Decree n°2012-928 dated 31 July 2012 has not deleted the requirement for the SARL to make two copies of the agreement available.

Board and Shareholder Approvals

[367] Where control of a company has been acquired, it will be necessary to hold a meeting of the shareholders to appoint the purchaser's representatives as members of the Board of Directors or Supervisory Board, as the case may be (or the purchaser's nominees as *gérant* in the case of an SARL, or *société de personnes* or *Président* for an SAS). In the case of an SA it may also be necessary to hold a meeting of the Board of Directors to appoint the new Chairman of the Board and the new *Directeur Général* or *Président Directeur Général* of the company.

[368] In the case of an SARL, French company law provides that the shares cannot be sold to a person who is not already a shareholder unless the proposed purchase has been approved by an extraordinary resolution of the shareholders passed by a majority of the half of the company shareholding (expect if the bylaws provides a higher majority). The proposed purchase must be notified by registered letter in advance to the company and to each of the shareholders: failure to reply within three months of such notification is regarded as implicit consent. If the company refuses to approve the proposed sale, the other shareholders or the company itself must acquire or cause the shares to be acquired within three months from the date of such refusal. The above provisions are mandatory and cannot be contracted out of.

[369] There is no comparable mandatory procedure in the case of an SA or in the case of an SAS. However the articles of association may lawfully contain a provision subjecting sales to a third party (or even to a shareholder in case of an SAS) to the prior authorization of the Board of Directors or the general meeting of shareholders. Where there is such a provision, the procedure to be followed in relation to a proposed sale of shares is identical to that outlined above for an SARL.

[370] Finally, where a parent company sells all of its interest in a subsidiary which represents a substantial part of its business, the courts may regard this as an implied change of activity entailing an amendment to the objects clause of the company. Any such amendment should of course be authorized by an extraordinary resolution of the shareholders passed by a two-thirds majority in an SA or an SCA (with the consent of the *commandités*), by the majority determined in the articles of association in an SAS, and in an SARL by a three-quarters majority (or two thirds if the company is incorporated after 2 August 2005). Failure to obtain such authorization may subsequently result in the transaction being invalidated by the court. It is therefore prudent, in borderline cases, to obtain the authorization of the shareholders in order to avoid any subsequent difficulties.

Transfer of Shares of Listed Companies

[371] The acquisition of a controlling interest in a listed company may be effected only through the procedure of the *offre publique* (takeover bid) with the possibility in certain cases of using a simplified procedure (*offre publique simplifiée*).

[372] By way of introduction, shares listed on a regulated market on the Stock Exchange can be traded on three different markets operated by Euronext Paris, a subsidiary of NYSE Euronext:

- *Eurolist Paris,* which is the Paris regulated market resulting from the merger in 2005 of the former first market (*premier marché*), the second market (*second marché*) and New market (*nouveau marché*).
- *Alternext Paris,* which is a market for small and mid-sized companies seeking to finance growth and gain access to the financial markets of the Euro zone.
- *Marché libre* (over the counter), which is not a regulated market where the company or any shareholder may require registration of the company (as the former *marché hors cote*).

Regulatory Overview

Supervisory Authority: The *Autorité des marchés financiers (AMF)*

[373] Except for the legal provisions of the Commercial Code and the Financial and Monetary code, the regulations referred to below are issued by the French financial market supervisory authority, the *Autorité des marchés financiers* or 'AMF', which is also in charge of supervising their enforcement.

[374] The company running the French Stock Exchange is Euronext Paris; however, the AMF is the administrative authority in charge of supervising all regulated markets in France.

[375] The AMF, which is comparable to the American SEC, was created in 2003 from the merger of the *Commission des Opérations de Bourse* (COB), the *Conseil des marchés financiers* (CMF) and the *Conseil de discipline de la gestion financière* (CDGF) (Financial Security Act of 1 August 2003 (Law No. 2003-706)). The AMF has broad duties to protect the markets and is authorized to issue rules and regulations, which are codified in the AMF General Regulation and its implementing instructions, as well as recommendations or positions. The AMF has wide investigative, disciplinary and other powers in relation to financial market operations.

[376] The powers vested in the AMF are exercised by:

- a Board (*collège*) of sixteen members, all of whom are appointed by public authorities (the chairman or *Président* is appointed by the President of the French Republic for a non-renewable five-year term), and
- an enforcement committee, a committee with exclusive powers to impose penalties and sanctions, with twelve members, who are not member of the Board. The chairman of the enforcement committee is elected by the members of the committee from among the four judges of the French High Courts (*Conseil d'Etat* and *Cour de cassation*) serving on it.

[377] The Board is assisted by specialized committees and consultative committees.

The Finance Minister designates a representative of the government who has a non-voting seat on all AMF bodies.

[378] The AMF has a staff headed by a Secretary General. The staff is composed of public servants under contract, private employees and public servants.

[379] The AMF is essentially responsible for:

- the protection of savings invested in securities or in any other public investments; the AMF accordingly gives clearance for the appointment of the managers of investment funds (for *sociétés d'investissement à capital variable* or SICAVs), for the establishment of *sociétés de gestion de portefeuilles individuels* (individual portfolio management companies) or for the publication of *notes d'information* in the context of a takeover bid;
- ensuring the provision of information to investors; and
- supervising the fair operation of the markets for securities, listed financial products or negotiable forward contracts.

[380] The AMF may propose to the government the modification of laws or regulations. It may also issue regulations (including the AMF General Regulations) recommendations, instructions or rulings (*rescrit*) and it has powers of investigation in respect of any activities which might be connected with criminal violations, such as insider trading.

[381] In order to enforce these powers, the AMF may impose sanctions such as injunctions or fines; it may also require the public prosecutor (*parquet*) to impose criminal penalties or to grant provisional injunctions against an infringing party, although it is not entitled to cause the prosecutor to initiate criminal proceedings.

[382] The AMF also lends its support to financial market regulation at the European and International levels.

Regulatory Overview

[383] The essential rules governing the purchase of shares in a listed company are contained in the AMF General Regulation, which is available on the website of the AMF, in French or in English (<*www.amf-france.org*>).

[384] The organization of the markets is being thoroughly changed by the implementation into French law of the EU Markets in Financial Instruments Directive (MIFID) due to come into force on 1 November 2007. The bulk of the new legislation has been introduced through restated articles of the Commercial Code and Financial and Monetary Code and of the AMF General Regulation (the executive order of 11 September 2007 approving the amendments to the AMF General Regulation was published in the French Republic official gazette on 27 September 2007). As noted by the Chairman of the AMF in his 2006 annual report to the President of the French Republic and to the French parliament implementing these sweeping reforms is bound to raise many questions in the coming months, while also creating new opportunities for financial intermediaries'.

[385] Pursuant to Article L.233-11 of the Commercial Code, any clause in an agreement which allows preferential terms and conditions to be applied to the sale and purchase of shares which are listed on a regulated stock market and which amount to at least 0.5% of the capital or voting rights of the company must be submitted within five days of the signing of the agreement to the issuing company and to the AMF. Failing such submission, the effects of that clause are suspended, and the parties are released from their undertakings while any public offer of sale is in progress. The company and the AMF must also be informed of the date on which the clause lapses. Furthermore the AMF General Regulation provides for the disclosure these clauses.

Takeover Bids (Offres Publiques or OP)

[386] There are two main types of takeover bids: the offre publique d'achat (OPA), where the consideration is in cash and the offre publique d'échange (OPE), where the consideration consists of shares of the bidder or a related company. Other possibilities include alternative offers whereby shareholders may decide if their shares shall be paid in cash or in shares and principal offers with one or more non-severable subordinated options.

[387] Pursuant to the act of 1 February 2011(Article L.433-4 of the Monetary and Financial Code), the *offre publique* is required for any breach of the threshold between 30% and 50% of the capital or voting rights. This process of takeover replaces the standing offer.

[388] Takeover procedures are closely supervised by the AMF. This supervision involves prior approval of the OP, the issue of information and notices to the public, monitoring of the target company and monitoring of the takeover transaction itself. The rules summarized below apply to both OPAs and OPEs.

[389] When the AMF has reasonable grounds to believe that a person is about to start an OP, it may request a declaration of intentions with regard to future purchases and strategy over the next twelve months.

Filing of the Draft Offer, the Information Notice and the Reply Document with the AMF

[390] The contemplated OP must be filed with the AMF by a bank or another financial institution which guarantees the irrevocability and due fulfilment of the undertakings of the company initiating the OP. It must contain the following information:

- the purpose of the OP and the intentions of the offeror at the time of filing;
- the number and characteristics of the shares in the target company already held by the offeror; and
- the price or exchange ratio offered, and the factors taken into consideration for establishing these (the AMF may request the offeror to review the price offered if it considers the price unacceptable on the basis of objective criteria).

[391] The OP must be made for 100% of the share capital and voting rights of the target company whereas, prior to May 1992 an OP could be made for not less than two thirds of the voting rights. The rule enacted in May 1992 was intended to protect minority shareholders and to maintain equal treatment of all shareholders. Subject to this rule, the offeror may make the offer conditional upon receipt of a stated percentage of shares, failing which the OP may be permitted to lapse.

[392] Exceptions to the requirement to offer for 100% of the share capital and voting rights are limited to:

- Offers initiated by a shareholder, or various shareholders acting in concert, holding the majority of the share capital and the voting rights of the target company;
- Offers initiated by a shareholder, or various shareholders acting in concert, targeting to acquire the majority of the share capital and the voting rights of the target company;
- offers restricted to 10% of the target company's share capital with voting rights, or voting rights, together with the offeror's existing shareholding (whether direct or indirect) and voting rights;
- offers initiated by an offeror, acting alone or in concert, for specific types of securities, such as preferred shares;
- repurchase offers initiated by the company with a view to cancellation of the shares for which the offer is made; an offer by the issuing company for securities giving access to its equity;
- offers initiated by the issuing company to exchange debt securities that do not give access to capital for equity securities or securities that do give access to its capital.

[393] Once the proposed offer has been filed, the Chairman of the AMF may ask the market operator that runs the regulated market on which the target company's securities are listed to halt trading in those securities. Such request may also extend to other securities concerned by the draft offer. If need be, the same request may be made to more than one market operator.

[394] The AMF shall have ten trading days from the beginning of the offer period to determine whether the draft offer complies with applicable laws and regulations.

[395] Pursuant to the act of 22 October 2010, the price of the offer must at least be equal to the higher price paid by the takeover bidder. The minimum price is the higher price paid during a twelve months period before the *fait générateur* (operative event) of the obligation to file an offer.

[396] If the draft offer complies with its regulations, the AMF will publish a reasoned statement of compliance that also constitutes an approval of the offer document. If the document does not meet the requirements, the AMF will refuse to issue a statement of compliance for the draft offer and will state the grounds for refusal. Where appropriate, the AMF will set a date when trading of the concerned securities shall be resumed if trading is still halted and will inform the market operator accordingly.

[397] Pursuant to Article 231-18 of the *Règlement Général de l'AMF*, amended by an order dated 31 January 2011, the company initiating the OP must also draft a *note d'information* (information notice) to be filed with the AMF containing information on:

- the identity and characteristics of the offeror;
- the offeror's intentions over the next twelve months regarding the industrial, financial and labour policy in the target company;
- employment guidelines of the offeror;
- the law applicable to contracts between the offeror and holders of the target company's securities following the offer, and jurisdictions;
- the agreements, if any, with respect to the OP to which the offeror is a party or of which it is aware;
- the terms of the offer, including in particular:
  (a) the proposed price or exchange ratio, based on generally accepted objective valuation criteria, the characteristics of the target company and the market for its securities;
  (b) the number and type of securities that it promises to acquire;
  (c) the number and type of securities of the target company that the offeror already holds directly, indirectly or in concert, or may hold on its own initiative, as well as the date and terms on which such holdings were acquired in the last twelve months or may be acquired in the future;
  (d) where applicable, the conditions to which the offer is subject;
  (e) the planned timetable for the offer;
  (f) where applicable, the number and type of securities tendered in exchange by the offeror;
  (g) the terms of financing for the transaction and the impact of those terms on the assets, activities and financial results of the companies concerned;

- if relevant, the opinion and the reasons of the Board of Directors or Supervisory Board, or, in the case of a foreign offeror, the competent governing body, regarding the benefits of the offer or the consequences of the offer for the offeror, its shareholders and its employees; and the voting procedures whereby this opinion was obtained, with the possibility for dissenting members to request that their identity and position be mentioned;
- if relevant, a report made by an independent appraiser;
- procedures for making available information about the legal, financial, accounting and other characteristics of the offeror and the target company.

[398] Once the offer period begins, the draft offer document is made available to the public.

[399] The target company must also draft an information notice to be filed with the AMF within five market days following the date of the publication of the reasoned statement of compliance by AMF. This information notice must contain a presentation of the company, a breakdown of its share capital, any shareholders' agreement of which the target company is aware, the independent appraiser's report in case of conflict of interest, the advice of the Board of Directors or Supervisory Board on the benefits or risks of the OP for the target company and for its shareholders, if available comments by the works council, whether members of the governing bodies intend to tender their shares into the offer, the procedures for making available the information about the legal, financial, accounting and other characteristics of the offeror and the target company.

[400] It should be noted that when the OP is a friendly takeover, a single information notice may be drafted by both the offeror and the target company.

Processing of the OP

[401] The OP starts with the publication of an *avis d'ouverture* (opening notice) made by the AMF and of any other French regulatory approvals which may be required (see above). The AMF may also publish an *avis* which states the offer was not accepted.

[402] The *avis d'ouverture* mainly specifies the number of shares which the offeror already holds, the minimum number of shares which must be delivered in response to the OP, the proposed price or exchange ratio and the closing date of the OP. In another document also called *avis*, Euronext specifies the conditions and timetable of the OP.

[403] The OP must be irrevocable and must remain open in principle for at least twenty-five market days until thirty-five days from the date of publication of the *avis d'ouverture*. The AMF may extend this period by postponing the closing date of the offer. In such case, the AMF publishes the new timetable for the offer. Selling orders given in response to the OP can be cancelled at any time during the period in which the OP remains open.

[404] The OP is then published by the AMF. If the OP has failed, the shares are returned to their owners.

[405] There is a basic difference between OPAs and OPEs as regards the ability of the offeror or of the parties acting in concert with it to conduct open market purchases during the OP. In an OPE, such persons are prohibited from acquiring shares of the target company, whereas they are allowed to do so in the case of an OPA if the offer is for 100% of the shares (except when the offer is conditional upon receipt of a stated percentage of shares). However if the price of the shares so purchased is in excess of the offer price of the OP, the offer price of the OP must automatically be increased by 2%.

[406] Competing OPs may be lodged with the AMF until five market days prior to the closing date of the initial OP. Where the AMF declares a competing offer to be compliant, it determines whether to postpone the closing date of the offer(s) and to void orders tendering securities to the earlier offer(s). Competing OPAs must be at an offer price of not less than 102% of the price per share of the initial OP, except where the competing OPA is not conditional upon a minimum number of shares being delivered in response to it (when the initial OP was subject to such a condition). As regards competing OPEs, the AMF merely considers whether the modifications brought to the offer are significantly better than the previous terms and whether an extension of the initial timetable is necessary.

[407] The initial offeror must indicate to the AMF its intentions (e.g., whether to maintain or cancel the OP or to modify its terms by a *surenchère*) at the latest five market days after the publication of the *avis d'ouverture* of the competing offer.

[408] The AMF may set a time limit for filing the successive competing offers when more than ten weeks have elapsed since the publication of the *avis d'ouverture* of the initial offer. This time limit may not be less than three market days from the date of publication of the decision rendering each competing offer official.

[409] Between the closing date and the result of the OP, the offeror and the persons acting in concert with it may not sell any of the shares received in response to the OP: they may purchase such shares only at a price equal to the offer price of the OP.

Mandatory OP

[410] Any person, whether acting alone or in concert with others, who holds directly or indirectly more than three tenths of the voting rights or share capital of a listed company (pursuant to Articles L.233-10 of the French Commercial Code), must file an OP with the AMF for 100% of the share capital and voting rights of the target company. The OP may not be conditional on presentation of a minimum number of shares. Such procedure is applicable to shares admitted on a regulated market.

[411] A mandatory OP must also be filed when any person, acting alone or jointly, holds directly or indirectly between three tenths and half of the voting rights or share capital of a company and increases such shareholding by more than 2% within a period of less than twelve consecutive months. This process is not required if the threshold exceeds 50% slowly and gradually. Such procedure is applicable on a regulated market.

[412] A mandatory OP must also be filed when a person, acting alone or jointly who holds 30% of the share capital or voting rights as a result of an acquisition or contribution which represents an essential part of the assets of the company absorbed. This procedure is applicable on regulated market.

[413] On unregulated market, any person acting alone or jointly who holds directly or indirectly 50% of the share capital or voting rights of the French company must file an OP if the market operator submits the procedure to the AMF.

[414] The AMF may decide the mandatory OP is not necessary if the case falls into exceptions, or if the AMF decides the definition of concert is not met, even if the person holds 30% of the shareholding.

[415] The AMF may grant exemptions from this rule where the one-third threshold is passed as a result of:

- a transfer for no consideration between individuals;
- a distribution of assets by an entity pro rata to its shareholders;
- a subscription to a share capital increase of a company in a situation which has proven to be difficult from a financial viewpoint, subject to the approval of the general shareholders' meeting;
- a merger or contribution of assets transaction subject to the approval of the general shareholders' meeting;
- a merger or contribution of assets transaction subject to the approval of the general shareholders' meeting accompanied by the execution between the shareholders of the relevant companies of an agreement constituting an action in concert;
- a reduction in the aggregate number of shares or in the aggregate number of voting rights in the company or a repurchase by a company of its own shares followed by their cancellation;
- the purchaser or a third party already holding the majority of the voting rights in the company;
- the redistribution by the purchaser of the shares between companies or individuals belonging to the same group;
- acquisition of the control of a company holding 30% of the share capital or voting rights of another company listed on a regulated market, providing the acquisition is

[416] It should be pointed out that the exemptions are not automatic. They are subject, in each case, to a decision of the AMF after review of the circumstances relating to the allocation of the share capital and voting rights and of the conditions under which the transaction, if any, was subject to the approval of the shareholders. The AMF may also give an exemption prior to completion of a transaction on the basis of its contemplated terms. In addition to the above-mentioned exemptions granted on a case-by-case basis the AMF may grant an exemption to the mandatory OP rules when the thresholds are crossed by one or several persons who declare they act in concert with (i) one or several shareholders who already hold alone or in concert the majority of the share capital or voting rights in the company (provided the latter remains prevailing) or with (ii) one or several shareholders who already hold alone or in concert between one third and one half of the share capital or voting rights in the company, provided that the shareholders maintain a higher participation and that they do not cross the thresholds of one third or 2% as a result of the action in concert.

[417] Pursuant to the Article 234-9 7° of the AMF General Regulation, the jurisprudence has decided on 15 September 2011 (in the case *Hermès*) that the Mandatory OP was not required when a family group holds 30% of the shareholding. The Court of Appeal decided the notion of intra-group transactions was filled because of the presence of a group of family shareholders controlling the capital of the Company.

[418] It should also be pointed that the parties may include a clause of *seuil de renonciation* (waiver threshold) under which the voluntary public offer does not succeeded. The person who wants to be part of the company must hold a shareholding determined in percent, in the respect of the principle of equal treatment among shareholders. This rule is only applicable to voluntary public offer and mandatory squeeze out as the jurisprudence decided in *Seloger* and *Valtech* cases.

Management of the Target Company

[419] The managers of the target company must conduct its corporate affairs in a prudent manner during the OP, in particular with respect to public comments, stock exchange transactions, and the use of the company's credit and assets. Any extraordinary decision must be notified to the public subject to the AMF's supervision. In addition, the management of the target company is not permitted to increase any existing cross-ownership percentages.

Conflicts of Interest

[420] Pursuant to Article 261-1 of the AMF General Regulation, the target company must appoint an independent appraiser if the transaction is likely to cause conflicts of interest within its Board of Directors, Supervisory Board or other governing body that could impair the objectivity of such governing body or jeopardize the fair treatment of shareholders.

Article 6. Supervision of the OP

[421] During the course of the OP, all companies involved, including their directors, shareholders holding at least 5% of the share capital or voting rights at ordinary shareholders' meetings of the target company, and any other person acting in concert with them, are required to disclose to the AMF, on a daily basis after the market has closed, all their transactions in the shares of companies involved in the OP.

[422] Pursuant to Article 231-46 I of the AMF General Regulation, amended by an order dated 10 July 2009, the same disclosure obligation rests on anyone who has acquired, since the beginning of the OP, more than 1% of the share capital or voting rights at ordinary shareholders' meetings of the target company.

[423] Any individual or legal entity that has increased the number of shares or voting rights that it holds in the target company by at least 2% of the total number of such shares or voting rights is required to make public its intentions with regard to a tender offer in progress. In case of change of intention, a new declaration must be forwarded to the AMF. Since the order of 19 July 2009, the declaration of intention is not required when any individual or legal entity has acquired a number of shares representing more than 5%, 10%, 15%, 20%, 25%, or 30% of the equity or voting rights of the target company.

[424] The AMF may require any *société de bourse* to disclose the identity of a client who has given a selling order and to make a client comply with the AMF General Regulation.

Offres Publiques Simplifiées (Simplified Procedure)

[425] In certain limited cases such as those described below, it is possible to use a simplified procedure, subject to the approval of the AMF:

- Offers initiated by a shareholder, or various shareholders acting in concert, holding the majority of the share capital and the voting rights of the target company. In such an event, the offered price shall not be lower than the average weighted market price for the sixty market days preceding the publication of the *avis de dépôt* of the OP;
- Offers initiated by a shareholder, or various shareholders acting in concert, targeting to acquire the majority of the share capital and the voting rights of the target company;
- offers restricted to 10% of the target company's share capital with voting rights, or voting rights, together with the offeror's existing shareholding (whether direct or indirect) and voting rights;
- offers by an offeror, acting alone or in concert, for specific types of securities, such as preferred shares or investment certificates;
- repurchase offers by the company with a view to cancellation of the shares for which the offer is made;
- repurchase offers by the company, quoted on a regulated market, of 10% of its shareholding;
- an offer by the issuing company to sell securities granting access to its equity;
- an offer by the issuing company to exchange debt securities that do not give access to capital for equity securities or securities that do give access to its capital.

[426] OPs subject to a simplified procedure must remain open for at least ten market days in the case of an OPA, for at least fifteen market days in the case of an OPE, as opposed to twenty-five market days for OPs subject to the standard procedure.

Article 8. *Offres Publiques de Retrait* (OPR)

[427] Pursuant to the Law of 2 August 1989 (see above), as modified by Law n°2010-10243 of 22 October 2010, shareholders of a company whose shares are listed on a regulated market (and on unregulated market since 1 February 2011) may ask for the shares of the company to be delisted from the regulated market under the following circumstances (Articles 236-1 et seq. of the AMF's General Regulation):

- When a person or persons acting in concert hold at least 95% of the voting rights of a company, then one or several minority shareholders may request the AMF to cause the majority shareholders to submit a public offer to purchase the shares held by the minority shareholders in the company. Upon receipt of this request, the AMF notifies the company and reviews the terms and conditions of the OPR with the company and with the financial institutions which will guarantee the due performance of the transaction. Even in cases where the majority shareholders hold 95% of the voting rights in the company, the AMF may nevertheless refuse to comply with the request of the minority shareholders, especially if it is of the opinion that the market in which the shares are traded is sufficiently liquid.
- When a person or persons acting in concert hold at least 95% of the voting rights at general meetings, one or several majority shareholders may also require the delisting of the company. In such a case, the OPR may be followed by the 'squeeze-out' procedure (*retrait obligatoire*) provided the valuation of the shares by an independent expert appointed by the initiator was approved by the AMF at the time the initiator submitted the OPR project to the AMF for approval. The shares of the company are then delisted when the OPR has expired (whatever its result may be) and the company is no longer regarded as a public company. However, it should be borne in mind that the AMF may refuse the delisting of the shares (see above). Since 1 February 2011, this procedure has been extended to companies whose securities are admitted on unregulated financial market as Alternext.
- When an SA is transformed into an SCA, the shareholders controlling the company must submit an OPR to purchase the shares of the minority shareholders immediately after the adoption by the general meeting of the resolution regarding the transformation. The initiator must specify in this case whether it will require the delisting of the shares, depending on the outcome of the OPR.
- When one or several controlling shareholders (e.g., the shareholders holding directly or indirectly the majority of the voting rights at general meetings or who control the company de facto) intend to modify significantly the company's articles of association or the company's activity, the AMF must then be notified of the proposed modification and will review with the controlling shareholders whether or not the implementation of an OPR is appropriate. A significant modification of the company's articles of association or the company's activity includes, pursuant to Article 236-6 of the AMF General Regulation, the transformation of the company, the modification of the conditions for transfer of shares, such as the insertion of an approval clause, and the transfer or contribution to another company of all, or the principle corporate assets. The AMF reviews the consequences of the proposed transaction as compared to the shareholders' rights and interests and sets forth, with the agreement of the controlling shareholders, the conditions of the OPR, such as the purchase price. It should be noted that the minority shareholders can

validly refuse the public offer submitted by the controlling shareholders unless the initiator has implemented an OPR followed by a mandatory delisting.

[428] The implementation of the OPR is subject to the same rules as those applicable to the *offre publique simplifiée* (see above). The AMF may require the offeror to draft a *note d'information* except when the offeror holds at least 95% of the voting rights of the company. In such case, the shareholders in a group of shareholders holding at least 95% of the voting rights must publish in a financial newspaper, no later than the day preceding the opening of the OPR, an announcement, subject to the supervision of the AMF, specifying how the purchase price was determined, the intentions of the purchasers, the circumstances of the transaction and the financing means.

Protection against Hostile Takeover Bids

[429] Protection in this particular field is tantamount to prevention, since once an OPA has been launched there is very little the target company can do, other than try to find a white knight. The Board of Directors or the Managing Board of the target company may implement a share capital increase based on authority delegated by the extraordinary shareholders' meeting, subject to compliance with the following conditions:

- the extraordinary shareholders' meeting must have expressly authorized the Board of Directors or the Managing Board to increase the share capital during the takeover bid;
- such authorization must have been given prior to the opening of the takeover bid and for the period between the dates of the ordinary shareholders' meeting;
- the share capital increase must not have been reserved for one or several specific persons.

[430] Pursuant to Article L 233-32 II of the French Commercial Code, the Board of Directors or the Managing Board of the target company may also issue warrants, which can be transferred at no cost to all of the shareholders of the Company during the offer period. This article does not apply to a foreign raider whose jurisdiction does not provide for an equivalent possibility.

[431] Preventive measures, in France as elsewhere, involve certain well-known techniques: the creation of stable groups of shareholders (*noyaux durs*), cross participations (which are prohibited in excess of 10%), the issue of securities convertible into shares (e.g., convertible bonds, bonds redeemable in shares, or bonds carrying subscription warrants for shares), the issue of shares carrying double voting rights (this is only possible where fully paid-up shares have been owned by the same shareholder for a minimum period of not less than two years) or the issue of shares carrying preferred dividends without voting rights and investment certificates without voting rights (neither of these categories may exceed 25% of the share capital).

[432] A company can also validly limit in its articles of association the voting rights attributable to each shareholder (by way of exception to the general principle that the voting rights attached to shares must be pro rata to their percentage of the share capital). This provision (resulting from the application of Article L.225-125 of the French Commercial Code) can even be inserted into the company's articles of association by an extraordinary shareholders' meeting held subsequent to the registration of the company. In the absence of statutory provisions relating thereto, the maximum number of voting rights can be freely determined within the articles of association: the maximum voting rights can correspond to a specific figure (such as hundred) or can decrease pro rata to the number of shares held; such provision may be limited to specific shareholders' meetings (ordinary or extraordinary, or to meetings with a specific agenda).

[433] Under French company law, the limitation must be imposed on all the shareholders, irrespective of the class of shares held (except for preferred shares without voting rights).

[434] Furthermore, provisions whereby shares held by a group of shareholders or by shareholders acting in concert are regarded as held by a single shareholder for the purpose of calculating the limitation on voting rights, should be unenforceable. Some companies whose shares are admitted on a regulated market have inserted in their articles of association another type of limitation on voting rights, whereby no shareholder can exercise his or her voting rights beyond a maximum percentage, irrespective of his or her shareholding.

[435] Although the limitation on voting rights is a deterrent to a potential raider unless the potential raider's shares can be spread out among friendly individual or corporate shareholders, this preventive technique entails drawbacks for the existing controlling shareholders, who are also subject to the same restriction as the potential raider.

[436] Some corporate forms such as the SCA are also appropriate when implementing a preventive measure against hostile takeover bids, for the reasons set out above.

[437] Finally acquisitions or sales of shares in companies with shares admitted on a regulated market must be notified to the company and to the AMF when certain percentages are reached. Thus a purchaser must inform the AMF within five days and the company within five days when the purchaser holds more than 5%, 10%, 15%, 20%, 25%, 30%, 33.33%, 50%, 66.66%, 90% or 95% respectively of the shares or voting rights. The obligation applies both to the purchaser (or the seller) and to other persons acting on the purchaser's behalf or in concert with him or her. Failure to notify entails a prohibition from voting the relevant shares for a period of two years starting from the notification. When a person holds more than 10% or 20% of the shares or voting rights of a company with shares admitted on a regulated market his or her intentions regarding future purchases of shares and strategy for the next twelve-month period must be declared to the AMF. A new declaration of intention must be established in the event of a change in the intentions declared initially which may only result from material changes in the environment, the situation or the shareholding of the relevant person.

Criminal Violations Relating to Listed Shares

Insider Trading

[438] Insider trading is punishable by criminal and administrative penalties which can be served consecutively.

[439] First, the criminal penalties. Pursuant to Article L.465-1 of the French Monetary and Financial Code, any insider (*initié*) and any person having access in the course of his or her professional functions to privileged information on the prospects or position of an issuer of securities admitted on a regulated market or on the prospects of a financial instrument admitted on a regulated market, who, before such information was made available to the public, carries out or causes to be carried out either directly or indirectly one or several transactions, may be sentenced to:

- a prison term of two years; and/or
- a fine of EUR1,500,000, which may be increased to up to ten times the profit on the trade, but shall never be less than the profit.

[440] These provisions also apply in relation to information on an issue of securities traded over the counter.

[441] Insiders may comprise and include all categories of persons subject to the supervision of the AMF under Article L.225-109 of the French Commercial Code, i.e.:

- the president, the directors and the general managers of an SA in the traditional form and in the form of a *Société Européenne*;
- the members of the Managing Board or Supervisory Board of an SA in the two-tiered form;
- the *gérant* and members of the Supervisory Board of an SCA;
- the spouses of the above-mentioned categories of persons.

Voting rights and dividend entitlements on shares hold by any person who does not fulfil requirements of Article L.225-109 of the French Commercial Code will be suspended until regularization. Any vote or payment of dividend made during this period would be null.

[442] It should be noted that in addition to these categories, any person having access through his or her professional functions to privileged information, (e.g., de facto insiders) even though such person is not employed by the company, is considered as a potential offender and may incur a penalty of one year's imprisonment and a fine of EUR150,000, which may be increased to up to ten times the profit on the trade, but shall never be less than the profit. When the insider is a legal entity it will be liable if the criminal offence was committed by its officers. The legal entity can, in such a case, be sentenced to the fine as prescribed above but equal to five times the amount of the fine applicable to individuals as well as to other penalties (such as dissolution, prohibition to conduct business for a maximum of a five-year period or for an unlimited period, prohibition from going public during a maximum of a five-year period or for an unlimited period). This liability of the legal entity is not exclusive of the liability which may be incurred by the officers. Furthermore, any person, other than those referred to previously, who knowingly obtains privileged information concerning the situation or the prospects of an issuer whose securities are admitted to trading on a regulated market or the likely performance of a financial instrument admitted to trading on a regulated market and directly or indirectly communicates that information, or allows it to be communicated, to a third party before the public has knowledge thereof, shall incur a penalty of one year's imprisonment and a fine of EUR150,000. If the information in question is used in the commitment of a crime or an offence, the sentence shall be increased to seven years' imprisonment and a fine of EUR1,500,000 if the amount of the profit realized is below that figure.

[443] The criminal offence may also result from purchase or sale orders traded on foreign stock exchanges whenever such orders were given from France.

[444] Article 465-1 of the French monetary code creates rather than a prohibition an obligation to abstain from trading during the period prior to the public disclosure of information. This obligation to abstain is reinforced by an obligation of confidentiality *vis-á-vis* third parties unaware of such information; in fact any person having access in the course of his or her professional activities and/or of his or her functions to privileged information who discloses such information to a third party outside the normal course of his or her activities may also be sentenced to a prison term of one year and/or to a fine of EUR150,000 equal to ten times the amount of the profit actually made by the insider, but which may in no case be lower than such profit.

[445] The insider must not necessarily have a fraudulent or speculative intention. It is sufficient if he or she acted or caused another to act with the knowledge that such information was not yet available to the public.

[446] In addition to criminal penalties, administrative penalties are incurred by people who use inside information they possess by acquiring or disposing of, or by trying to acquire or dispose of, for their own account or for the account of a third party, either directly or indirectly, financial instruments to which that information relates.

[447] Such persons must also refrain from:

(a) disclosing such information to another person otherwise than in the normal course of his employment, profession or duties, or for a purpose other than that for which the information was disclosed to them;
(b) advising another person to buy or sell, or to have bought or sold by another person, on the basis of inside information, the financial instruments to which such information pertains or any related financial instruments.

[448] The abstention requirements set forth in this article do not apply to transactions effected in discharge of an obligation that has become due to acquire or sell financial instruments, where such obligation results from an agreement entered into before the person concerned held inside information.

[449] Such abstention requirements shall apply to any person holding inside information by virtue of:

(a) membership in the administrative, management or supervisory bodies of the issuer;
(b) holdings of the issuer's capital;
(c) access to such information through the exercise of his employment, profession or duties;
(d) participation in the preparation or execution of a corporate finance transaction;
(e) activities that may be characterized as crimes or offences.

[450] These abstention requirements apply also to any person who holds inside information and who knows, or should know, that it is inside information.

[451] Where the person referred to herein is a legal entity, these abstention requirements also apply to individual taking part in the decision to effect the transaction on behalf of the legal entity.

[452] Pursuant to Article L.621-15 III of the French Monetary Code. When the above prohibitions are infringed, the AMF can sentence, through its own jurisdiction and through the *Commission des sanctions*, the offenders to a fine up to EUR100,000,000, which amount may be increased to a figure representing up to ten times the amount of any profit realized and which may not be less than the amount of that profit, even thought there is still a debate on whether the EUR100,000,000 sanction should be considered as a cap for the AMF or not.

False or Misleading Information

[453] Pursuant to Article L.465-2, subparagraph 2 of the French Monetary and Financial Code, any person who knowingly circulates to the public by any means false or misleading information on the prospects or position of an issuer of securities or on the prospects of a security or an asset defined in Article L.421-1 of the French Monetary and Financial Code, so as to influence the price of such security, is punishable by the same criminal penalties as those applicable to the use of privileged information or insider trading.

[454] Furthermore, the offence is constituted in any case of a wilful dissemination to the public of any inaccurate, untrue or misleading information regarding the issuer of the securities or the securities themselves. Any person responsible for such dissemination may be subject to fines.

Influencing the Price of a Security

[455] Any person who wilfully carries out (whether directly or indirectly) or attempts to carry out on the market where a security is listed an act intended to influence the normal operation of the market by deceiving another party may be subject to a prison term of two years and/or to a fine of EUR1,500,000, it being understood that this amount may reach a maximum of ten times the profit actually made. Article L.465-2 of the French Monetary and Financial Code deals specifically with this offence. The liability of the legal entity can be held liable in the conditions described under above.

[456] Alongside criminal prosecution, the AMF can sanction such behaviour under its jurisdiction, through the *Commission des sanctions*, and is entitled to order fines of fine up to EUR100,000,000, which amount may be increased to a figure representing up to ten times the amount of any profit realized and which may not be less than the amount of that profit.

[457] It shall be noted that provisions of law n° 2013-672 of 26 July 2013 introduced specific provisions in order to protect the market against high frequency trading practices.

Notification of Transactions

[458] The following persons shall notify the AMF of all acquisitions, transfers, subscriptions and exchanges of securities of any entity carrying out public offerings as well as the financial instrument transactions associated with it:

(a) members of the management or supervisory bodies of such entity;
(b) any person who has the power to make management decisions within the issuer and also has regular access to privileged information which directly or indirectly concerns such entity;
(c) persons having close personal links with the persons referred to above.

TAX CONSIDERATIONS

General Overview

Corporate Income Tax

[459] Under the territoriality principle, industrial and commercial profits generated by a commercial company or by an individual carrying on industrial and commercial activities are liable for French tax if earned in France and/or if taxation of such profits is permitted by or provided for under an international tax treaty. In application of specific anti-avoidance rules, income earned outside France by some controlled foreign companies may become taxable in France.

[460] Corporate income tax (the standard rate of which is equal to 33.33% and is increased by a 'social' surtax of 3.3% payable by corporations which corporate income tax liability exceeds EUR763,000 and, as the case may be, by an additional surtax of 5% due by companies which turnover exceeds EUR250,000,000) is imposed on the income received by SAs, SASs, SCAs and SARLs. A reduced rate of 15% applies to the first EUR38,120 of profits of small or medium-sized enterprises and this companies are exempt from the 3.3% surtax mentioned above. As an exception, when an SARL has one shareholder who is an individual (in such case, it is called an EURL) or several individual shareholders of the same family, it is not subject to corporate income tax (unless the shareholder(s) so elect(s)) and profits are then taxed in the hands of each of the individual shareholder(s) according to his or her individual tax regime. The SARL is then said 'tax-translucent'. Other SARLs, as well as SAs, SASs and SCAs, can also elect, under certain conditions and for a limited period of time, to be 'tax-translucent', in which case their taxable income remains determined at their own level but is taxed in the hands of their shareholders,

[461] SNCs, GIEs and *sociétés en participation* are excluded from the scope of corporate income tax unless they exercise an option for liability to corporate tax. These partnerships are 'tax-translucent' for French tax purposes, i.e., each of the partners is subject to taxation on the portion of the income derived from the company according to his or her or its individual tax regime.

[462] Profits attributable to the *commandités* of an SCS are taxed in their hands, whereas the portion of profits attributable to the *commanditaires* is always subject to corporate income tax at the company's level.

[463] French branches of foreign companies are liable for corporate income tax as the French tax principle is that earnings from an establishment operated in France are subject to corporate tax in France. Furthermore, a French branch of a foreign company will be subject to a 30% withholding tax on its after-tax profit deemed to be distributed, unless a tax treaty reduces or eliminates this withholding tax or unless it can be proved that no distribution of dividends occurred. A 3% distribution tax may in addition be due on the same after-tax profit deemed to be distributed.

[464] Apart from corporate tax, there is an annual minimum company tax which is due by all entities subject to the payment of corporate income tax and whose turnover is more than EUR15,000,000. This tax varies from EUR20,500 to EUR110,000 depending on turnover of the entity concerned (EUR110,000 being applicable to entities whose turnover exceeds EUR500,000,000) and is due irrespective of the profit or loss position of the company concerned. This annual minimum company tax should no longer apply as from 1 January 2014.

Tax Losses Rules

Tax Losses Carry-forward

[465] Losses incurred during a tax year may be carried forward indefinitely, provided that the activity carried out by the company having generated these losses does not change dramatically. Save for specific exceptions, the amount of tax losses that can be deducted in a given year is limited to EUR1,000,000 increased by 50% of the portion of taxable income of the company exceeding this threshold.

[466] In the context of mergers, losses of the absorbed company generated before the effective date of the merger cannot be transferred to the absorbing company unless a special authorization is granted by the Ministry of Economy and Finance (which authorization may not be refused if certain conditions are met).

Tax Losses Carry-Back

[467] Companies may also carry back losses incurred in the financial year of the election against the undistributed profits of the last financial year. The amount of tax losses that can be carried-back every year is limited to EUR1,000,000. The excess tax income deemed to have been paid after carrying back losses is available as a tax credit against payment of corporate income tax due over the subsequent five years and is reimbursed after this period if not allocated to the payment of the corporate income tax.

Business Capital Gains

[468] Capital gains realized by companies, whether on a short-term or a long-term basis are taxed in principle at the standard corporate income tax rate.

[469] However, several exceptions exist for certain long-term capital gains. The major one relates to capital gains resulting from the sale of participatory securities (shareholdings of more than 5% held for at least two years in companies which assets are not predominantly composed of real estate assets not used for business purposes). 88% of capital gains on sales of such securities are exempt from corporate income tax. Conversely, capital losses arising from disposal of these securities and depreciation allowances booked in relation thereto are not tax deductible. Capital gains resulting from the sale of participatory interests (shareholdings of more than 5% held for at least two years) in companies which in companies whose assets are predominantly composed of real estate assets not used for business purposes are subject to corporation tax at the standard rate, except if these companies are listed, in which case the capital gains are subject to corporation tax at the reduced rate of 19%.

[470] Capital gains realized by individuals or companies which are not subject to corporate income tax are taxed as follow:

- short-term gains (i.e., capital gains realized on assets which were purchased or created for less than two years) are taxed according to the seller income taxation rate;
- long-term capital gains (i.e., capital gains realized on assets which were purchased or created for more than two years) are taxed at the rate of 31.5% (16% plus additional taxes).

Taxation of Dividends

At the Level of the Distributing Company

[471] Distributions made by French companies to French-resident beneficiaries are not subject to any withholding tax. A withholding tax is conversely levied on distributions made to non-French resident beneficiaries (at a rate of 30%, increased to 75% if the beneficiaries are acting through a so-called non-cooperative jurisdiction). However, the withholding tax may be reduced (sometimes to 0%) in application of a number of rules (including double tax treaties, EU Directives, etc.), provided that the conditions required for these rules to apply are met. Since August 2012 a 3% specific tax is also payable by French entities (which do not qualify as small-and-medium-sized enterprises) which pay dividends (and assimilated distributions, including as the case may be excess interest on loans granted by direct shareholders) to French and non-French resident beneficiaries (other than entities which are members of the same consolidated tax group). The 3% specific tax is not a withholding tax per se and thus cannot be reduced or eliminated in application of the above mentioned rules. It is not deductible for corporate income tax purposes.

At the Level of the Recipient Company

[472] Dividends are in principle subject to tax at the standard corporate income tax rate. As an exception, when a French holding company subject to corporate income tax, a branch or a permanent establishment of a foreign company for at least two years in France owns at least 5% of the shares of another French or foreign company the dividends (and corresponding foreign tax credits as the case may be) received from the subsidiary are then exempt from corporate income tax in the hands of the parent company under the affiliation privilege, save for a fraction equal to 5% of the aggregate proceeds of the dividends received (including foreign tax credits as the case may be). As a consequence of this exemption, the foreign tax credits attached to these dividends cannot be deducted from the corporate income tax due from the parent company (but only, under certain conditions from the withholding tax due when the dividends are re-distributed by the recipient company to its own foreign shareholders).

Taxation of Interest

[473] Interest expenses incurred by companies are tax-deductible for corporate income tax purposes (on an accrual basis) to the extent that the corresponding financings have been contracted in the direct interest of the companies and that the conditions of such financings (including the interest rates charged) are 'normal'. The tax-deductibility of interest may however be limited by the application of a number of specific rules (some of which are detailed below).

[474] French thin-capitalization rules limit the tax deduction of interest due by French companies under loans granted by 'related entities' (i.e., companies that control or are controlled by the borrowing company or the same persons as the borrowing companies) and loans granted by third-parties but guaranteed by 'related entities' (up to a portion which depends on the nature and value of the securities granted by the related entities).

Where applicable, thin-capitalization rules provide (cumulatively) for the following:

- interest is deductible only if the share capital of the borrowing company is fully paid-up;

- the maximum rate of deductible interest is a specific rate published by the tax authorities every quarter or, if higher, the rate that the borrower could have obtained from independent financial institutions in a similar situation, i.e., a 'market rate' (interest rate test);
- interest that may be deducted for tax purposes is limited to a maximum amount which takes into consideration (i) a 1.5/1 debt/equity ratio, (ii) a cap equal to 25% of operating profits before tax, interest paid to related parties and depreciation allowances and (iii) the total amount of interest received from related parties (thin-cap test).

The limitations described above apply only if 'excess interest' exceeds EUR150,000. Certain adjustments allow disallowed interest to be carried forward within certain limits. No limitation applies to interest paid by entities whose debt/equity ratio is lower than that of the group of companies to which they belong. Specific neutralization rules are also provided for in respect of interest paid between companies that are members of a same tax group and safe harbour provisions prevent the above rules from applying to cash pooling entities and credit institutions.

Interest due by French companies under loans granted by direct shareholders that are not also 'related entities' to the borrowers is tax-deductible only up to the specific rate published by the tax authorities every quarter and mentioned above.

[475] The tax-deduction of interest expenses borne by all members of a consolidated tax group is limited in the case where a member of such group acquires (for a cash consideration) shares in a subsidiary from a 'controlling party' and that subsidiary subsequently enters into the consolidated tax group to which the purchasing company belongs. Where this rule applies, a portion of interest expenses born by all the members of the consolidated tax group in question (determined on the basis of the cash consideration paid to acquire the subsidiary and the average amount of debts of the group members) is added-back to the taxable income of such tax group during a maximum period of nine years.

[476] The tax-deduction of interest incurred by a company in relation with the acquisition of a participating shareholding interest in a subsidiary is also limited if the purchasing company is not able to demonstrate that this shareholding interest is 'managed from France' (i.e., that the decisions related to this shareholding interest are made in France and that the control or influence over the acquired subsidiary is exercised from France). In this case, a portion of interest expenses borne by the purchasing company (determined on the basis of the cash consideration paid to acquire the subsidiary and the average amount of debts of the group members) is added-back to its taxable income during a maximum period of nine years.

[477] If the net financial expenses incurred during a given tax year by a company (or by all members of a consolidated tax group, as the case may be) exceed EUR3,000,000, such net financial expenses are tax-deductible up to 85% of their amount only (the non-deductible portion being increased to 25% from and including 2014). The non-deductible portion of financial expenses is not available for carry forward.

[478] Interest paid by French companies is not subject to any withholding tax, unless it is paid to beneficiaries acting through a so-called non-cooperative jurisdiction (in which case a 75% withholding tax is levied).

Tax Consolidation (Intégration Fiscale)

[479] A tax consolidation regime is applicable, without requiring prior approval from the Ministry of Economy and Finance, under certain conditions, which are discussed below.

Qualifying Conditions and Tax Consolidation Parameters

[480] Any French holding company subject to French corporate income tax under standard rules, whose share capital is not held at least as to 95% directly or indirectly by another company subject to French corporate income tax, may elect to become the sole taxpayer liable to corporate tax due on the consolidated results of the group existing between the French holding company and those of its French subsidiaries in which it holds directly or indirectly at least 95% of the voting rights and share capital (the tax consolidation perimeter).

[481] It is not possible to include within the tax consolidation regime a subsidiary held by another subsidiary which itself is not a group member, even if all conditions for its inclusion are met, and except if the interposed company is situated in the EU and controlled at more than 95% by the French parent company. A tax-consolidated group may however only include French companies subject to French corporate tax at the full standard corporate income tax rate. Members of a group must close their financial years on the same date.

[482] In order to benefit from this tax regime, a foreign company holding directly or indirectly French subsidiaries may either set up a French holding company or register its shares on the balance sheet of a permanent establishment in France considered to be the parent company and liable for all the tax obligations of the French group. The French holding company must have elected for this tax regime for a minimum five-year period.

[483] In order to benefit from this tax regime, a foreign company holding directly or indirectly French subsidiaries may either set up a French holding company or register its shares on the balance sheet of a permanent establishment in France considered to be the parent company and liable for all the tax obligations of the French group. The French holding company must have elected for this tax regime for a minimum five-year period.

Determination of the Group Taxable Result

[484] The group taxable result is determined by the French holding company. A group result corresponds to the algebraic sum of the results of each of the tax-consolidated companies, as previously determined and declared according to ordinary rules as if they were separate taxpayers. In particular, each company determines its own net long-term capital gains or losses.

[485] Any losses incurred by each company before the application of the tax-consolidation regime is only deductible from its own subsequent profits (tax loss carry-forward against profits/capital loss carry-forward against long-term capital gain). However, this should not be considered as a disadvantage since the situation would be the same if the option for the tax-consolidated regime had not been exercised.

[486] The consolidated tax result determined by the holding company is the sum of the taxable results of each group member subject to the following adjustments:

(a) Any double taxation or double deduction disappears. Therefore, any reserve for bad debts booked on receivables held by a tax-consolidated company *vis-à-vis* another tax-consolidated company must be added back into the group result. Similarly, any depreciation for shares booked by the holding company *vis-à-vis* its tax-consolidated subsidiaries must also be added back into the group result.
(b) Forgiveness of debts and direct or indirect subsidies granted between companies of the group are not taken into account in determining the group result. Any indirect subsidy must be identified and neutralized whenever a fixed asset of a tax-consolidated company is transferred to another tax-consolidated company at a price which is different from its market value. However, this rule does not apply when the assets transferred are portfolio shares excluded from the long-term capital gains regime.
(c) Capital gains or losses resulting from the sale of assets between group members are excluded when determining the group taxable result for the financial year in which the sale took place.
(d) When shares in a company which becomes a member of the tax-consolidated group are acquired from the group's direct or indirect shareholders, a portion of the group's overall financial charges is added back to the group's taxable result. This provision even applies if the acquiring company does not borrow funds to finance the acquisition of the shares (the so-called *Charasse* amendment). This restriction does not apply when the shares are acquired from a third party or from the group's direct or indirect shareholders if it can be proved that the group's shareholders have themselves acquired the shares from an unrelated party with the sole intention of reselling them immediately to the company.

Impact of a Tax-Consolidated Company Leaving the Group

[487] When a company ceases for any reason whatsoever to be a member of the group, there are certain adverse tax consequences. The departing company cannot carry forward the losses incurred while it was a member of the group against profits generated after its departure. These losses are definitively transferred to the group. All the subsidiaries of the departing company also cease to be members of the group. The results of the departing company will not be taken into account in the results of the group as from the starting date of the on-going fiscal year during which the departing company ceased to be a member of the group.

[488] Any subsidy resulting from the difference between the transfer price of an asset and its real market value must be added back to the group result of the year when the company benefiting from such transaction leaves the group. The previous capital gains or losses on intra-group sales of assets are added back.

[489] Any other subsidies and forgiveness of debts must be added back to the group result for the year in which the company benefiting from this transaction leaves the group, but only to the extent they have been deducted from the group result of one of the five preceding years. No recapture is necessary after this five-year period.

Payment of Group Tax Liability

[490] When electing for the tax-consolidation regime, the holding company becomes the sole taxpayer of the group although each member of the group remains jointly and severally liable for the payment of the tax due (for the portion it would have paid in the absence of tax consolidation) should the holding company be in default.

[491] The holding company can set off, against the corporate income tax due in respect of the overall group result, the aggregate annual minimum corporate tax of all the group members even if some of the members generate net tax losses.

Article 6. Taxation of the Sale of a 'Fonds de Commerce'

[492] The sale of a *fonds de commerce* is subject to transfer tax (*droit de mutation*) on the higher of:

- the purchase price of the tangible and intangible assets transferred; or
- the fair market value of the tangible and intangible assets transferred. The transfer tax (deductible for tax purposes) is reduced to nil on any amount below EUR23,000 and its rate is 3% for the portion of the purchase price/value ranging from EUR23,000 to EUR200,000 and 5% for the portion of the purchase price/value over EUR200,000. The sale of inventories is not subject to the transfer tax.

[493] If the sale of a fonds de commerce entails the conveyancing of a commercial building, the purchaser must pay:

- if the sale does not fall within the scope of VAT the standard transfer tax at the effective rate of 5.09% (to which a specific 0.1% registration fee and notary fees should be added),
- VAT at the standard rate of 19.6% plus a registration duty at the rate of 0.815%, if the sale falls within the scope of VAT. It should be noted that the standard rate of VAT should be 20% as from 1 January 2014.

Either VAT or registration duties are assessed on the purchase price of the property assets (or their fair market value if higher) increased by any other consideration due to the seller.

[494] The sale of a *fonds de commerce* triggers capital gains taxation for the seller in ordinary conditions in respect of each asset transferred.

Tax Treatment of Mergers and Acquisitions

Taxation of Mergers

[495] A *fusion* (merger) or *scission* (spin-off) implies the winding-up of the absorbed company and a contribution in kind to the absorbing company. The application of general tax rules to these transactions entails a tax burden on each company which would make their implementation extremely unattractive. The importance of merger transactions for the national economy has led to the enactment of more favourable tax rules in relation to *fusions*. For the same reason, the *apport partiel d'actif* also benefits from special tax rules similar to those applicable to *fusions*. Under these special tax rules, the transaction is treated as if no change had occurred regarding the business transferred and the absorbing company is deemed to conduct the business of the absorbed company in lieu of the latter without any break. These special rules only apply to companies subject to corporation tax. Where the absorbing company is a foreign company, the benefit of these special rules is subject to obtaining a prior authorization (*agrément*) from the French Ministry of Economy and Finance. These special rules provide for exemptions in the field of company tax, personal income tax, registration duty and value added tax.

Corporation Tax

[496] Both *fusion* and *scission* imply the winding-up of the absorbed or contributing company. The latter should accordingly be subject to corporation tax on the profits of its current fiscal year, and those relating to previous fiscal years whose taxation has been deferred as well as on capital gains resulting from the transaction. However, under the special tax rules applicable only to the *fusion*, the contribution may be exempt from capital gains tax related to both moveable and non-moveable assets and the absorbed company will only be taxed on the profits relating to its current fiscal year and on any provisions which are no longer justified. The benefit of these special rules is conditional upon the absorbing company making a number of commitments. It must:

- add back over a maximum five-year period (or fifteen-year period in relation to buildings) into its taxable profits all capital gains on depreciable assets;
- calculate the capital gain relating to the resale of non-depreciable assets by reference to the value they had in the accounts of the absorbed company;
- enter in its accounts the provisions and the long-term capital gains reserves of the absorbed company.

[497] Where the transaction is a *scission* or an *apport partiel d'actif*, the benefit of the special tax rules is subject to an approval given by the French Ministry of Economy and Finance. However the approval is not required for an *apport partiel d'actif* regarding a *branche complète d'activité* (i.e., assets able to be organized as a business which can work on its own) provided the contributing company undertakes, in the *apport partiel d'actif* agreement, (a) to retain for a period of three years the shares of the receiving company remunerating the contribution, and (b) to calculate the capital gain relating to the resale of the shares of the receiving company by reference to the value of the contribution in the accounts of the contributing company.

[498] No prior approval of the French Ministry of Economy and Finance is required for a *scission* when all of the following conditions are met:

- the split-up company had at least two distinct business activities (e.g., two branches);
- the companies to which the business lines were distributed each received one or more branches of the dissolved company's activities; and
- the shareholders of the split-up company receive a pro rata share of the survivor companies' shares (in principle, this condition may not be satisfied, because as a general rule the aim of a *scission* is that each shareholder of the split company receives shares of one only of the survivor companies and not of each of them) and agree to hold them for at least three years.

[467] When an *apport partiel d'actif* is placed under the common regime it must be considered as a sale of assets taxable under the regime of business gains such as referred to above. Although this common regime is not frequently applicable, an *apport partiel d'actif* may be placed under this regime when the contributing company has large tax losses carried forward which may offset the capital gains which it will make under the contribution or when the contributing company wants to sell the shares received in exchange for its contribution immediately after the contribution. Another advantage of the common regime lies in the fact that the receiving company will benefit from an upgraded basis for depreciation.

Taxation of Shareholders

[499] The allotment of shares of the absorbing company to the shareholders of the absorbed company is not, under the special rules, regarded as taxable income. Where the transaction is an *apport partiel d'actif*, the allotment of shares of the benefiting companies to the shareholders of the contributing company is also not regarded as taxable income, provided that this allotment of shares is completed within one year from the contribution and is approved by the French Ministry of Economy and Finance.

[500] Furthermore, the capital gains resulting for the shareholders of the absorbed company from the exchange of shares can be rolled-over if certain conditions are met (taxation being then deferred until the time the shares allotted by the absorbing company are sold).

Registration Duty

[501] Mergers and scissions are registered at a fixed rate of EUR375 or EUR500 (depending on the amount of the share capital of the benefitting company). Where the contribution is an *apport partiel d'actif* of a complete and autonomous branch of activity (*branche compléte et autonome d'activité*), it may also be registered at the same limited cost. No prior approval of the French Ministry of Economy and Finance is required for a contribution related to a complete and autonomous branch of activity. Otherwise, standard transfer taxes are payable (depending on the nature of each asset transferred).

[502] The favourable regime related to registration duty is entirely independent from the tax regime related to corporation tax (see above). It is therefore possible to place the contribution within the favourable tax regime from a registration duty viewpoint, whereas the contribution comes under the normal regime from a corporation tax viewpoint.

[503] The contribution of real property under a *fusion* or contribution of a *branche complète et autonome d'activité* is exempt from any transfer tax but may trigger the payment of notary fees, VAT and a 0.1% or 0.815% registration duty.

Value Added Tax (VAT)

[504] Where the transactions imply companies which are all subject to VAT, the transfer of the assets of the absorbed/contributing company is exempt from VAT. Its VAT credit can be transferred to the absorbing company provided the latter undertakes to make the regularizations which were required from the absorbed company. Otherwise, VAT is applied in ordinary conditions to the transfer of every asset falling within its scope.

Share Acquisition

Taxation of the Sale of Shares

[505] The sale of shares in an SARL, SNC, SCI and SCS is subject to a registration tax of 3% of the purchase price after application of a deductible of up to EUR23 000 (depending on the portion of shares sold). The sale of shares in an SA, an SAS or SCA is subject to a registration tax of 0.1% of the purchase price.

[506] However, with shares of SA or SCA admitted on a regulated market, the registration tax of 0.1% is only due if the transfer is recorded in a document. The transfer of shares of French companies listed on the stock exchange and whose market value exceeds EUR1,000,000,000 is subject to a specific transaction tax (*taxe sur les transactions financières*) at a rate of 0.2%. The *taxe sur les transactions financières* is tax deductible for corporate income tax purposes.

[507] It results from the above tax rules that a share acquisition is subject to a more favourable transfer tax treatment in France – especially for the transfer of shares in an SA, an SAS or in an SCA – than an asset acquisition (see above).

[508] Capital gains earned by selling shareholders are subject to personal income tax or corporate income tax, as the case may be, subject to specific rebates / reduced rates applicable in certain conditions.

Taxation of the Sale of Shares Held in Real Estate Companies

[509] In the case of sale of shares in a company (irrespective of its corporate form) which shares are not admitted on a regulated market and which assets are directly or indirectly composed for more than 50% (in value) of real estate investments, the applicable transfer tax is equal to 5%, assessed on the market value of the underlying real estate, reduced only by the outstanding amount of debts of the company having initially financed the acquisition or construction of such real estate.

[510] Capital gains earned by corporate shareholders upon disposal of shares in non-listed real estate companies are always subject to corporate income tax at the standard rate (i.e., the affiliation privilege does not apply).

[511] A specific 3% tax is payable every year by any entities (whether companies, organisms, trusts or similar institutions with or without legal personality) which own French property, either directly or indirectly. However, a number of investors benefit from an exemption, including international organizations, sovereign States, entities which French assets are composed directly or indirectly for less than 50% (in value) of French property, entities which shares are significantly and regularly traded on a regulated market, entities whose head office is in France, in the EU or in a country that has concluded a treaty with France providing for administrative assistance or entitling them to benefit from the same treatment as French entities and (i) which share in French property that they own directly or indirectly represents less than EUR100,000 or less than 5% of the market value of that property or (ii) which are pension funds or which carry out non-for-profit activities of public interest and necessitating the investment in French property or (iii) which are certain collective investment funds or (iv) which disclose every year the identity of their own shareholders or members to the tax authorities. When due, the 3% tax is assessed on the market value of the French real estate assets and any entity in the holding chain which is interposed between the assets and the taxpayer are jointly liable for the payment of the tax.

LABOUR LAW ENVIRONMENT

[512] This section discusses the issue of the prior consultation of the Workers' Council (*Comité d'Entreprise*) in the context of merger and acquisition transactions, the transfer of employment contracts under merger and acquisition transactions and conditions for the application of Article L.1224-1 of the French Labour Code and finally Labour law issues regarding applicable rules to small- and large-scale collective dismissals based on economic grounds.

The Workers' Council

Consultation of the Workers' Council

[513] As per Article L. 2322-1 of the French Labour Code, a Workers' Council is mandatory within any company with a workforce exceeding forty-nine employees. The Workers' Council is composed of elected representatives of the employees, the number of whom varies according to the size of the staff. In companies with several plants or branches, a separate committee called a Local Workers' Council (*Comité d'établissement*) has to be set up in each plant or branch and a Central Workers 's Council must be implemented at the company level.

[514] The Workers' Council meets regularly (at least once a month) and has to be informed (and sometimes consulted) on the economic activities and situation of the company, on working conditions and safety and generally on all questions relating to employment. The new law of 14 June 2013 has introduced an obligation to implement a social and economic data base to be accessible to employee representatives (including trade union delegates) and covering certain items such as investments, shareholder equity and debts, officer compensation, etc. The precise content shall be specified by decree. The law has also created a new obligation to consult the Workers' Council on the company's strategic orientation in terms of activity and employment. In this context, the Workers' Council could be assisted by an expert and the Workers' Council opinion will have to be provided to the company's board. The social and economic data base shall be the support of this new consultation.

[515] With specific regard to acquisitions, Article L. 2323-19 of the French Labour Code defines some of the situations which render compulsory the information and/or the consultation of the Workers' Council: the consultation must be implemented in the event of a modification of the economic or legal organization of the employing company, such as a merger, acquisition, or transfer of business (hereinafter the 'transaction'), as well as in the event of purchase or a sale of subsidiary; the employer must also consult the Works Council when the company (incorporated in France) takes a share interest (whatever its size) in another company; the employer will only need to inform the Works Council when he/she knowledge of the taking of a share interest in the company. In addition, according to Article L.2323-6 of the French Labour Code, the Workers' Council must be informed and consulted on any change relating to the organization, management, or general running of the business, in particular where the anticipated measures affect the size or the structure of the work force, working hours, or employee's terms and conditions of employment, working conditions, or access to vocational training.

[516] Case law renders compulsory the consultation of the Workers' Council in situations where the transaction significantly impact on the employees' status or entails a change of control of the employer. Accordingly, the situations where an employer must consult its Workers' Council need to be reviewed on a case-by-case depending on the transaction and its consequences.

Case law renders also compulsory information and consultation of Health and Safety Committee, in relation to any project having expected changes on working conditions. The Health and Safety Committee is mandatory within any company with a workforce exceeding forty-nine employees pursuant to Article L.4611-1 of the French Labour Code.

[517] One should note that the Workers' Council must also be informed when a tender offer or a exchange offer (*offre publique d'achat offre publique d'échange*) is filed: Articles L. 2323-21 and subsequents of the French Labour Code renders compulsory the information of the Workers' Council both of the target company and of the offeror immediately after the filing of such takeover exchange. In this situation, the Workers' Councils of the target may require the offeror to appear at one of its meeting to supply additional details and to answer questions. However, a draft bill is currently discussed before the French Parliament, which shall amend substantially the above mentioned provisions. According to the draft bill, Article L.2323-23 of the French Labour Code shall be modified to provide the consultation of the Workers' Council of the company prior to any proposed tender offer (whether amicable or not). Such consultation would occur prior to the decision taken by the Board of Directors on the proposed tender offer under the conditions provided by Article L.2323-3 of the French Labour Code (see below in this respect). The author of the tender offer will have to be informed of the opinion of the Worker' Council, which shall also be included in the note of information prepared by the author of the tender offer and the target company for the AMF. Current proposed amendments of the draft bill also provide a process of follow up of any undertaking taken by the author of the tender offer over the next three years following completion of the offer.

[518] One should also note that when a company is involved in concentration transaction, its Workers' Council must be informed within three days after the publication of the filing to the French or European competition authorities pursuant to Article L.2323-20; this information procedure needs to be implemented even if the Workers' Council has already been consulted prior to the transaction in accordance with Articles L. 2323-6 or L.2323-19 of the French Labour Code. However, this information procedure is not required when the Workers' Council has been informed in the context of a takeover bid or a takeover exchange.

[519] The consultation process must be conducted with the Workers' Council or the Central Workers' Council. (In certain circumstances, the Local Worker's Council may have to be also consulted, in particular when the transaction has a specific impact on the employees of the plant concerned. The Group Worker's Council is only consulted in the case of tender offer or exchange offer concerning the leading company of the group.)

[520] However, this consultation may have to be implemented before the Staff Delegates (*Délégués du Personnel*) under certain conditions. (Where the company employs more than fifty employees and no member of the Workers' Council was elected at the last elections, the employer has to inform and consult the Staff Delegates (if any) in the same conditions as the Workers' Council.) The same rule will apply in relation to the Health and Safety Committee, in the absence of candidate to the election of this Committee, the Staff Delegates shall be consulted on the measures affecting the working conditions of the employees.

[521] In order to comply with French labour law, the consultation of the Workers' Council must be organized by the employer prior to the decision to execute the documents relating to the transaction and before the transaction has become final. French case law provides that the employer must first consult the Workers' Council on the reorganization of the company (i.e., legal, economic, financial aspects) and then on the consequences of such reorganization for the employees.

[522] It must be stressed that when the transaction entails job diminutions and redundancies, a specific consultation procedure will need to take place; this specific consultation procedure will depend on the number of positions whom elimination is envisaged.

The draft bill currently discussed before the French Parliament provides for an obligation of prior information of the employees in the event of sale of majority shares or capital stake, if the company has less than 250 employees. This obligation shall not apply to companies over 250 employees, or to companies in bankruptcy proceedings and to companies transferred by way of succession or other related family transfers. Failure to respect such obligation could entail the nullity of the transaction made in breach of employees 'right. The draft bill provides also measures to facilitate the purchase of such companies by the employees.

Timing of the Consultation Procedure

[523] A new law of 14 June 2013 has amended rules regarding consultation procedure applicable as from 1st July 2013 subject to implementation of decree of application. It must take place as soon as the employer has sufficient information about the transaction to inform completely and fully the Workers' Council and before the transaction has become irreversible. The offence of 'obstruction' is committed when the parties reach an agreement on the main elements of the transaction without previously consulting with the Workers' Council, if the transaction is deemed to be definitive in 'principle' even though its implementation is not yet effective.

[524] Article L.2323-3 of the French Labour Code provides that the time period during which the Workers's Council must provide its opinion on the transaction should be defined by an agreement between the employer and the Workers' Council. Failing which, the time period will be fixed by a decree, which is not yet enacted, and could not be less than fifteen days.

In view of the drafting of these new provisions, it is understood that at least two meetings shall be required to complete the consultation procedure.

Pursuant to Article L.2323-4 of the French Labour Code, the Workers' Council must be provided with precise and written information to enable its members to study and appreciate the reasons, modalities and consequences of the transaction, and to express its opinion. The opinion does not need to be positive and the Workers' Council has no right of veto. If the members of the Workers' Council consider that the information provided is insufficient, they could initiate an action in summary proceedings before the President of the Civil Court in order to obtain communication of missing information. The judge must render its decision within eight days and therefore, the duration of the consultation procedure is not extended due to this judicial action.

At the expiry of the above-mentioned time period, the Workers' Council is considered as having been consulted and rendered a negative opinion if it refuses to vote.

[525] The agenda for the consultation meeting must be communicated to the Workers' Council at least three days prior to the meeting and eight days before the meeting in the case of the Central Workers' Council. The required information must be given to the Workers' Council sufficiently ahead of time so that it has enough time to analyse the contemplated transaction.

[526] Furthermore, the Workers' Council may appoint any expert or auditor to help it assess the company's situation before taking a view on the proposed transaction.

The new law fixed the conditions under which experts assisting the Workers' Council must provide their report. The time period granted to the expert to provide its report must also be agreed with the Workers' Council, failing which it will be fixed by a decree yet to be published.

Sanctions for Failure to Consult

[527] Failure to comply with the obligation of prior information and consultation of the Workers' Council constitutes a criminal offence called *délit d'entrave* (obstruction), sanctioned by a maximum fine of EUR3,750 and/or in theory, by a maximum of one year imprisonment for the employer (i.e., the authorized representative of the company, generally the chairman of the company) and a maximum fine of EUR18,750 for the company itself.

[528] In addition, the employer who fails to consult the Workers' Council is exposed to summary proceedings in front of a civil Court. In this course of action, the Workers' Council can ask for the stopping of the transaction until its members have been properly informed and consulted.

Transfer of Employment Contracts under Merger and Acquisition Transactions Conditions for the Application of Article L. 1224-1 of the French Labour Code

Principle of Transfer of Employment Contracts

[529] Pursuant to Article L. 1224-1 of the French Labour Code, in the event of a modification of the legal situation of an employer, in particular, by way of succession, sale, merger, change in the structure of the business, transformation into a company, all of the employment contracts in force on the date of the modification shall continue to exist between the new employer and the employees of the business.

[530] On the basis of this article and implementing case law, the transfer of all or part of the assets of a company will not affect the employment relationship and all employment agreements will be automatically transferred. Such a transfer would fall within the scope of Article L. 1224-1 of the French Labour Code only if it occurs in the context of the transfer of 'an autonomous economic entity, maintaining its identity and continuing or resuming its activity' as defined by the French Supreme Court (*Cour de cassation*). Article L. 1224-1 could also apply in case of a partial transfer of a business/company, if such part of business/company could constitute by itself an 'autonomous economic entity' and if the part of the activity which is transferred, maintains its identity after the transfer.

[531] Article L. 122-12 paragraph 2 of the French Labour Code will not apply in the context of the sale of the shares of a company. From a Labour law point of view, the sale of the shares of a company is not considered as a modification of the legal situation of the company. As a result, we consider that there is no change of employer, thus there is no transfer and no consequence for the employees and their conditions of work. Of course, after the change of control, the new shareholder is free, under certain conditions, to reorganize the activity or the workforce of the company.

[532] Article L. 1224-1 is of public policy and cannot be waived. Refusal by an employee to transfer when Article L. 1224-1 lawfully applies could constitute a valid ground for dismissal for serious misconduct.

Exceptions

[533] Article L. 1224-1 will not apply in several circumstances:

- the elected corporate officers (*mandataires sociaux*) who do not have an employment agreement and thus are not subject to Labour laws, would not automatically transfer;
- the employees whose activity is related to the assets that are not transferred would not transfer;
- the employees whose activity is partly related to the transferred assets can only be transferred for part of their activity;
- in circumstances where only part of the assets are transferred, the transfer of 'protected employees' (i.e., to say in particular elected employee representatives, candidates to such offices, former employee representatives, union delegates) will be subject to the prior authorization of the Labour inspector.

Dismissals

[534] In theory, the employer is entitled to make redundant employees who are dedicated to the transferred activity prior to the implementation of the transaction if these redundancies are justified by economic reasons requiring job suppressions and if these redundancies do not aim at avoiding the application of the Article L. 1224-1 of the French Labour Code. However, such dismissals are rarely held valid by French Labour Courts except in situations where the economic situation of the employer renders necessary, as a matter of urgency, the job suppression before the transaction.

Consequences of the Transfer of Employment Contracts

[535] In accordance with Article L. 1224-1, the employment agreements are pursued at the same conditions (e.g., same functions, remuneration, classification, seniority, etc.), the only change being the change of employer.

[536] However, the maintenance of collective bargaining agreements and/or internal collective agreements in situations where Article L. 1224-1 paragraph 2 applies obeys certain rules. Pursuant to Article L. 2261-14 of the Labour Code, the collective agreements (collective bargaining agreement, internal collective agreements) should be pursued by the new employer as long as new collective agreements have not been negotiated, or at least, during one year. This article also provides for a three-month notice period for the collective agreements to be denounced. Thus, except if new agreements are negotiated during this period, the collective agreements stay in force for a total period of fifteen months.

Procedure for Collective Redundancies Based on Economic Grounds

[537] This section covers French Labour law issues regarding applicable rules to small and large-scale collective dismissals based on economic grounds.

[538] There are two categories of collective redundancies based on economic grounds:

- 'small' redundancies (i.e., redundancies of up to nine employees); and
- 'large scale' redundancies (i.e., redundancies of more than ten employees).

[539] Among those categories, there are three types of redundancies depending on the size of the company:

- redundancies of two to nine employees in a company with fifty employees and over;
- redundancies of more than ten employees in a company of less than fifty employees; and
- redundancies of more than ten employees in a company of fifty employees and over.

[540] Those redundancies are governed by French labour law subject to (i) possible additional provisions of the applicable collective bargaining agreement, if any and (ii) company-wide collective agreements that would be more favourable to the employees than the law or the relevant collective bargaining agreement.

The collective dismissal procedure has been substantially modified pursuant to a law of 14 June 2013, applicable since 1 July 2013, although some decree must still be enacted on certain issues.

Common Legal Requirements

[**541**] A preparatory phase calls for the following legal requirements, which are applicable to all categories of collective redundancies.

Grounds for Dismissal

[**542**] Under French Labour law, the company must be able to justify a proper economic cause. Dismissal for economic reasons (*licenciement pour motif économique*) is defined in Article L. 1233-3 of the French Labour Code, as resulting from 'the elimination or transformation of an employment position or modification of employment contract [. . .] notably as a result of economic difficulties or technological changes'. A dismissal based on economic grounds requires that the following two conditions be met: (i) the effective elimination or transformation of the work performed by the employee, or modification of the employment contract and (ii) the existence of economic reasons.

[**543**] Pursuant to case law, economic reasons (not tied to the performance of the concerned employees) shall refer to justifications based on either economic difficulties (only serious economic difficulties such as material financial losses, deterioration of the company's turnover), technological changes (only if the implementation of such changes has consequence on the work reorganization) or the reorganization justified by the need to safeguard the competitiveness of the company's business or of the company's sector of activity of the group to which it belongs. Court considers also that the closing of a company constitutes an autonomous cause of termination, subject to the absence of fault or blameful thoughtlessness of the company or group to which it belongs with respect to this decision.

The law of 14 June 2013 has not directly modified the definition of grounds for economic dismissal. It has however introduced a new regime applicable in the event of modification of employment contract resulting from collective agreement to maintain employment (*accord de maintien de l'emploi* or agreement on employment continuity) and of mobility (*accord de mobilité*). The first above-mentioned agreement must provide a commitment of the employer to maintain jobs of the concerned employees during the period of the agreement in counterpart of concessions from these employees in terms of remuneration, working time or organization.

The change provided by these agreements must be approved by the employees concerned. In the event the employee refuses the changes resulting from such collective agreement, the dismissal is qualified as economic. The qualification as an economic dismissal of these new collective agreements allowing a flexibility in employment however raise uncertainties as to the control of the judge on the ground justifying dismissals resulting from the application of such collective agreements. Indeed, a mobility agreement could be concluded within the scope of the general organization of the company. As far as agreements to maintain employment are concerned, the law states that these agreements could be concluded in the context of serious cyclical economic difficulties, which diagnostic must have given rise to a mutual assessment between the employer and the employee representatives, eventually assisted by an expert appointed by the Workers' Council.

In terms of procedure, only the rules of procedure of individual economic dismissal shall apply, and not of collective redundancies, even if more than nine employees refuse the change in their employment.

Redeployment Search (obligation de reclassement)

[544] The employer who intends to make redundant one or several employees must seek redeployment solutions within the company or within the group to which the company belongs: it implies that the employer must offer the employee, whose redundancy is contemplated, any available position within the company or the group (to the extent indeed such available position corresponds to his/her professional skills). Pursuant to Article 1233-4-1 of the French Labour Code, in the event of a group having companies in foreign countries, the employer must have asked the employees prior to dismissal whether he/she wants to receive redeployment offer in the countries concerned and subject to which conditions in terms of remuneration and place of work. The mobility questionnaire must be sent to the employees, in the event of collective redundancies, after the last meeting of the employee representatives and the employees have six working days from the date of reception of the questionnaire to answer. Failing to answer, the employee is deemed to have refused receiving any redeployment offer in a foreign country.

Failure to comply with redeployment search will expose the employer to pay damages for unfair dismissal to the dismissed employee. (If the employee made redundant shows that a position was available which he/she could have held and was not offered, his/her redundancy could be held unfair by the Labour court.)

Criteria for Redundancy Selection

[545] Unless they are determined by the applicable branch collective bargaining agreement, the criteria for selecting the employees to be made redundant shall be determined after consultation with the employee representatives. The employer is required by law to take into consideration all of the following criteria: family charges (in particular those of single parents), seniority, situations of employees whose re-engagement would be particularly difficult (such as disabled or aged people) and the employees' professional capacity per category. (Those criteria may be altered by the relevant collective bargaining agreement.)

[546] The employer is free to favour one of those criteria or to add other criteria as long as they all have to be determined and applied in an objective manner and that it applies all the legal criteria.

Specific Obligations

[547] In addition to the above-mentioned legal requirements, the employer will have to comply with specific obligations, with respect to each type of redundancy and actions may vary depending on the size of the company (i.e., implementing a social plan).

[548] The procedures, which main steps are described below, assume that:

- company has employee representatives bodies (either a Workers' Council or Staff Delegates);
- the Workers' Council may appoint any expert or auditor to help it assess the company's situation; and
- the company only has one site (if the company had several sites in France, the procedure would be more complex, due to the obligation to apply the selection criteria throughout the company at each site, even if the redundancies concerned only one site, except if agreed differently by collective agreement).

Redundancies of Two to Nine Employees in a Company of Fifty Employees and Over

[549] Such procedure will not concern more than nine employees and is less heavy for the employer since it does not require the implementation of any social plan, (the so-called *plan de sauvegarde de l'emploi*).

[550] Consultation requirements: the information and consultation process requires two steps prior to the implementation of the redundancies.

[551] Convening the members of the Workers' Council (or the Staff Delegates if there is no Workers' Council) to a first meeting by sending a letter which shall be:

- accompanied by a document setting out (i) the economic difficulties encountered by the company, (ii) the economic justifications for the redundancies, and (iii) the reasons why such redundancies will help the company's financial position. The Workers' Council shall also be provided with financial data enabling it to appreciate the company's situation, the number of contemplated redundancies, professional categories in question, criteria for redundancy selection, number of employees in the company and contemplated redundancy schedule.
- received sufficiently in advance (the French Labour Code provides for a minimum three-day notice but in practice, the staff representatives should be allowed a longer notice).

[552] Meeting with the members of the Workers' Council and consulting them on the proposed redundancies. They shall express an opinion and should this opinion be negative, it would not prevent the employer from implementing the redundancies.

[553] The new law extends the powers of review by the labour authorities of collective redundancies of less than ten employees and provides that these authorities control, within a period of twenty-one days following the notification of the dismissal, that the employee representatives have been duly consulted, that the employer complied with the redeployment obligation and implementation of relevant social measures. In addition, the labour authorities could make observations to be taken into consideration by the employer. This new provision raises a practical difficulty as a prior notification phase is not provided for in the French Labour Code for this size of redundancies.

The Redundancy procedure: once the consultation process is over, and assuming the Labour authorities duly notified did not make any observations, the employer is entitled to carry out the redundancy procedure as follows:

- The employer must first obtain from the Pôle Emploi (French unemployment organization), the *Contrat de Sécurisation Professionnelle (CSP)*), which may enable the employees to register for advance redeployment measures with that organization. (The CSP, which has a maximum duration of twelve months, aims at allowing dismissed employees to benefit from training and skills assessment operations in order to encourage their job finding, and provides a better unemployment coverage during the twelve months period. Should the employee agree to such CRP, he would not be entitled to a notice period indemnity since such compensation (in lieu of notice) is paid to the unemployment organization to fund this scheme. However, such compensation is paid only up to three months of pay so that employees entitled to a notice period beyond three months receive the balance of the compensation in lieu of notice.)
- The employer must sent the mobility questionnaire referred to above to the employee, who has six working days from the date of reception of the questionnaire to answer. Failing to answer, the employee is deemed to have refused receiving any redeployment offer in a foreign country.
- The employer needs then to convene each employee to a preliminary meeting (at least five working days prior to the date of the meeting) by registered letter which must indicate the purpose, date, time and place of the meeting; the employee can be assisted by a representative of his or her choice (such as an employee's representative, any employee of the company or an outside advisor).
- A preliminary meeting is then held with each employee (at least five working days after receipt of the letter): the purpose of which being to explain the reasons for its contemplated redundancy to the employee and in particular the economic grounds for the suppression of his position. Any available position (which could avoid the redundancy) as well as, depending on the size of the company, any opportunity to benefit from a Redeployment Programme, the so-called *Congé de Reclassement* or a CSP, shall be offered to the employee during the meeting. (For companies with 1,000 employees or more (and companies belonging to a group with more than 1,000 employees in France or in certain European countries), a 'Redeployment Programme' which cannot exceed twelve months, has to be offered to employees whose redundancy is being contemplated. For companies with fewer than 1,000 employees, the CSP has to be offered to each employee whose redundancy is being contemplated with at least one year of seniority. The employee may accept the CSP scheme within a maximum of twenty-one days following receipt of the documents. If the employee accepts the CSP, the contract of employment is terminated at the end of the twenty-one days period. It is therefore recommended to provide the reason of the envisaged termination in the letter given to the employee at the time the CSP is proposed. At the end of the contract, a maximum of three months of salary out of the notice period (which the employee

does not perform) are paid over to the unemployment organization to fund the CSP, as well as the employee accrued right to individual training.

- The employer will have to notify the termination (not before a seven-working day period since the meeting) by sending the redundancy letter (by registered mail with acknowledged receipt and which shall set out the precise cause for termination) to the relevant employee. The redundancy letter is considered as a conservative measure until the expiry of the above mentioned twenty-one days period to accept or refuse the CSP, if one has been proposed. If the redeployment programme called *congé de reclassement* applies, it should be stated in the dismissal letter and the employee has eight days from the receipt of the dismissal letter to opt for it.
- The employer must inform the local Labour Authorities (Labour Inspector of the Department) of the redundancies made within a maximum of eight days following the sending of the redundancy letter.

Redundancies of Ten Employees or More in a Company of Fifty Employees and Over

[554] Those redundancies call for similar requirements as set out above with respect to economic justifications and redeployment obligation but require the implementation of a social plan, the purpose of which is (i) to attempt to avoid making the staff redundant in as much as possible by providing job-saving measures (part-time work, redeployment) or (ii) help the employees find alternative employment by providing assistance such as professional training or outplacement and/or (iii) compensate the employees' loss resulting from their redundancy by paying them additional damages. (

[555] The law of 14 June 2014 has modified the conditions of implementation of social plan, and in particular has simplified the procedure, which however entails more involvement of the labour authorities. The law has also introduced an obligation of research of a buyer in the event of closure of a site.

According to the new provisions, the employer has two possibilities to implement such collective redundancies:

(i) either the company concludes a collective agreement with the majority trade unions; or
(ii) the company determines the content of its social plan on an unilateral basis.

According to an instruction from the Labour Ministry dated 26 June 2013, the labour authorities must encourage the implementation through a collective agreement.

Collective Agreement

- Pursuant to Article L.1233-24-2 of the French Labour Code, the agreement determines the contents of the social plan, i.e., the measures proposed to reduce the projected redundancies and their effect, as well as the modalities of consultation of the works council. In this respect, the agreement could determine the scope and weight of criteria for redundancy selection, the calendar of implementation, the number of positions concerned, the modalities of implementation of the redeployment measures.

However, the law expressly states that the agreement could not depart from certain rules (such as the obligation of redeployment, redeployment programme or professional securing contract (*CSP*), general rules of consultation of Workers' Council).

- This agreement could be negotiated concomitantly to the consultation of the Worker's Council on the reorganization plan and its consequences on employment pursuant to Article L.1233-30 of the French Labour Code.
- The start of the negotiation must be notified to the competent Labour authorities (Direccte).
- The trade unions could appoint an expert to assist them during the negotiation process, which must be paid by the employer.
- To be valid, the agreement must be signed by one or several trade unions having got at least 50% of valid votes in favour of trade unions at the first round of the last elections of titular members of Workers' Council, or single delegation of personnel, or failing which of the employee delegates.
- The agreement must be ratified by the Labour authorities (Direccte), which shall control:
  (a) The conditions of conclusion of the agreement and its validity to the majority rule.
  (b) The compliance of its content to legal provisions.
  (c) The presence in the social plan of measures allowing to avoid or reduce the number of suppression of positions.
  (d) The validity of the procedure of information and consultation of the Workers' Council and Health and Safety Committee if required.
- The Direccte has fifteen days from the date of reception of the signed collective agreement to motivate its decision of ratification or refusal.
- In the event of refusal of ratification by the authorities, the employer must present a new agreement after having included the appropriate modification and having consulted its Workers' Council.

Unilateral Plan

- In such a case, the unilateral plan is established by the employer after the last meeting of information and consultation of the Workers' Council.
- The content of the plan is similar to the one provided for the collective agreement.
- The document must be sent after the last meeting of the Workers' Council to the competent Direccte, which has twenty-one days further to its receipt to approve the unilateral plan. In the event of refusal of approval, as for the collective agreement, the employer must present a new plan after having made the appropriate amendments and consulted the Workers' Council.
- In its new role, the Direccte shall control:
  (a) the compliance of the social plan contents to the legal and conventional provisions,

(b) the regularity of the consultation procedure of the relevant employee representative bodies (Workers' Council, Health and Safety Committee),
(c) the existence in the social plan of measures allowing to avoid redundancies or to limit its number, as well as redeployment measures.

In order to appreciate the contents of the social plan, the Direccte must take into account certain criteria, among which:

(1) the means available to finance the plan within the company, the social and economic unit or the group, as the case may be;
(2) the measures in light of the size of the restructuring;
(3) the redeployment and adaptation efforts made by the employer.

Any recourse against the decision of the Labour authorities could be made before the administrative court within two months following this decision. The Court should render its judgment within a three-month time limit.

According to the new provisions, the redundancies could not be notified to the employees before the expiry of a time period of thirty days further to the notification of the decision (approval or ratification), by the labour authorities or at the end of the period of review.

The new law introduces also new rules in terms of consultation of employee representatives.

As before, the Workers' Council must be consulted on the proposed reorganization, and its consequences, as well as on the proposed redundancies, although if the employer has concluded a collective agreement in this respect, it does not need to consult it on the points having given rise to this agreement. Indeed, a former consultation on the draft collective agreement shall have been made before signing such an agreement with the trade unions.

The Workers' Council members must be convened at a minimum two successive meetings separated by a fifteen-day period. Contrary to the former provisions, the law provides a maximum time period for the consultation of the Workers' Council of two to four months depending on the number of employees to be made redundant. Questions of the members must be answered by the employer during this time period.

Furthermore, the Workers' Council members may decide to appoint an auditor of their choice to assist them in understanding the reorganization and its consequences and in forming their opinion on the restructuring. The auditor must present his report at the latest fifteen days before the expiry of the time period mentioned above for the Worker's Council to express its opinion.

The law specifies that the health and safety committee should be consulted if the plan is composed of measures affecting the conditions of work of the employees. However, it simplifies the consultation process in the event the project concerns several sites by the appointment of a coordination health and safety committee. In such a case, only one expert could be appointed by the coordination committee within the same time period as mentioned above for the expert of the Workers' Council.

Redundancies of Ten Employees or More in a Company with Less than Fifty Employees with Staff Delegates

[556] Those redundancies are governed by similar requirements (see above with respect to economic justification, redeployment obligation and criteria for redundancy selection).

[557] Consultation requirements: As the company employs less than fifty employees, the employer does not have to prepare a social plan. Two steps are required.

[558] Convening the Staff Delegates: The letter convening the Staff Delegates to the first meeting must be accompanied by a document setting out:

- the economic, financial or technical reasons justifying the termination (i.e., a financial and economic note on the company);
- the number of planned redundancies;
- the professional categories in question;
- the criteria for redundancy selection;
- the number of employees in the company; and
- the planned redundancy schedule.

[559] Meeting with the Staff Delegates and consulting them on the proposed redundancies, as regards to the information they have been provided with. The employer has to convene the Staff Delegates to two meetings, the time period between those meetings may not exceed fourteen days. The information provided to the Staff Delegates as well as the minutes of each meeting must be communicated in the same time to the Labour Authorities. (These minutes must mention the Staff Delegates' remarks and proposals concerning the proposed redundancies. The Labour authorities will make sure that the Staff Delegates have been informed and consulted on the proposed redundancies.) and have a twenty-one day period to review the process and the measures provided by the employer from the date of notification of the redundancy project to the Labour Authorities (after the first meeting with the Staff Delegates). Redundancy procedure: notification of the termination requires that the redundancy letter may not be sent before a thirty-calendar day period since the date of notification of the redundancy project to the Labour Authorities.

[560] The redundancy of employees whose age exceeds fifty years old in the context of redundancies of more than nine employees should be carefully considered. The Labour Authorities indirectly supervise the redundancies of this type of employee and they can validly reject a social plan failing to provide for serious provisions concerning the placement of this type of employee.

Individual Training Rights and Re-engagement Priority

[561] Training rights: the law dated 4 May 2004 introduced the individual training right (*droit individual à la formation* – DIF) which enables all employees with at least one year of seniority to acquire 20 hours of professional training per year, (in principle outside working time), which may be grouped up to a maximum of 120 years over 6 years (subject to more favourable provisions of the applicable collective bargaining agreement). (The 20 hours are prorated for part time employees who may still group the hours up to a maximum of 120 hours. The employees need to have one year of service in the company to benefit from the DIF but those under a fixed-term contract only require a length of service of four months over the past twelve months.)

[562] In the event of a collective redundancy procedure, if the employee takes the CSP, his acquired DIF rights are paid directly to the French unemployment organization. The law requires the dismissal letter as well as the certificate of employment (to be given at the end of the contract) to mention the employees' rights accrued in this respect.

It should be noted that the new law of June 2013 has implemented a new training scheme (the personal account of training or *compte personnel de formation*) which shall replace the DIF in January 2014. The DIF rights should be transferred and capitalized in hours in this personal account, which could be used by the employees for training.

[563] Re-engagement priority: Employees made redundant have a right to a re-engagement priority. The employees have twelve months following the legal date of termination of the employment contract in which to inform the employer whether or not they wish to benefit from such a right. If they do, their priority right will cover the same period of one year from the legal date of termination of the contract and extend to all positions available in the company which the employee is capable of holding (even at a lower level, on a part-time basis or for a fixed term), during a one-year period. This priority only covers the former employing company and not other companies in the group. Failure to comply with that obligation would result in damages for the employee equal to at least two months' salary upon two conditions: the employee shall have at least two years of seniority in a company with a workforce exceeding eleven employees.

Protected Employees

[564] In addition to the common procedure (as explained above), a specific procedure applies to protected employees (in particular employees' representatives (including trade union representatives)) requiring (i) a specific meeting with the employee representatives pursuant to which the members as well as the protected employees to be made redundant shall vote. It shall be noted that a potential negative vote would not prevent the company from pursuing the redundancy procedure and (ii) an authorization from the Labour Inspector. In the absence of authorization of the Labour Inspector, the protected employees may not be made redundant.

French Labour Code provides also protection against redundancies for pregnant women, and women under a maternity-leave, which may limit their redundancies over a certain period of time.

Search for a Buyer in the Event of Closure of the Site

[565] In the event a company, which falls within the scope of the Redeployment Programme, called Congé de Reclassement, envisages to close a site, it shall proceed to the research of a possible buyer. In this context, the employer has an obligation to inform the Workers' Council of its research (including the proposed offer if any) and the Workers' Council has a right of control of such research with the help of an expert. A new bill is currently discussed before the Parliament under which this research would become an obligation subject to a fine of up to twenty times the minimum monthly wages should the employer refuses to sell the site to a serious potential buyer.

Bankruptcy Proceedings

[566] The new procedure applicable to mass redundancies have been adapted in such case:

- when redundancies are carried out in the event of safeguard plan (*plan de sauvegarde*), the common rules mentioned above apply (unilateral plan or collective agreement), except as follows: the Labour Authorities has a reduced period of eight days to approve the plan or the agreement as from the last meeting of the Workers' Council. In the case of refusal of the plan or agreement by the authorities, the employer must consult its Workers' Council within a three-day period, and amendment of the plan should be sent to the Labour Authorities, which has a new period of three days to answer.
- when redundancies are carried out over the observation period ('*période d'observation*') (i.e., the period during which a legal administrator reports on whether or not the company should be maintained), the legal administrator has to follow the rules exposed above before the bankruptcy judge approves the redundancies. The decision of the Labour authorities, as well as the opinion of the Workers' Council must be provided to the bankruptcy judge.
- in the context of rehabilitation proceedings ('*redressement judiciaire*') or if the company is to be liquidated (*liquidation judiciaire*), the legal administrator or the liquidator must negotiate a collective agreement or present an unilateral plan, and the employees' representatives must be consulted on the proposed redundancies and the Labour Authorities must be notified. However, the time period provided for the consultation of the Workers' Council in common proceedings shall not apply. In addition, the period of review by the Labour authorities to approve the plan is reduced to eight days in the event of *redressement judiciaire* and to four days in the event of *liquidation judiciaire*.

[567] Under the above-mentioned conditions (see paragraph above), a CSP shall be offered to the employees to be made redundant even during the bankruptcy proceedings.

The rules regarding the guarantee of salaries debt have also been revised to provide that the AGS (the unemployment protection organization in bankruptcy proceedings) covers the sums due to the employees resulting from the termination of their employment occurring during a twenty-one day period further to the liquidation judgment (instead of fifteen days) and extend the coverage to the social measures provided in the collective agreement or unilateral plan.

Article 10. Failure to Comply with the Above-mentioned Requirements

[568] Criminal offence: Failure to consult the employee representative bodies or pursuing the proposed redundancies in the absence of a formal vote constitutes a criminal offence, the so-called *délit d'entrave* (obstruction). Pursuant to the French Labour Code, such offence is sanctioned by a fine up to EUR3,750 and/or, in theory, a maximum of one-year imprisonment (the prison sentence is not indeed, in practice, applied for a mere lack of consultation) for the employer (i.e., the authorized representative of the company, generally the chairman of the company), and a fine up to EUR18,750 for the company.

[569] Challenge of the validity or the regularity of the procedure before the Labour court: is governed by the following statutes of limitations:

- If the dismissal letter expressly mentions that the employee benefits from an individual right to challenge the validity or the regularity of the procedure carried out against him, he may do so before the Labour court, but only within a twelve-month period as from the date of the dismissal.
- In the event of a CSP, the employee could challenge the termination of his/her employment contract within a twelve-month period as from the acceptance of the CSP, and assuming this information has been provided in the letter proposing the CSP to the employee.
- Failing such indication in the dismissal letter (such indication being optional), the employee is entitled to claim damages for abusive dismissals and payment of severance indemnities over a two-year period as from the date the employee concerned has known or should have known the facts allowing him/her to exercise his/her right.,.

Article 11. The Redundancy Costs

[570] Such costs refer to:

- the legal cost of the redundancies to be incurred by the employer (such as notice period, severance pay and paid vacation indemnities); and
- the damages that the company may be ordered to pay by a court (or at which it may decide to settle out of court) in the case of an unfair dismissal. The new law, subject to decree of application, introduce an indemnity scale according to the seniority of the employee to encourage settlement before the Court at the stage of the conciliatory hearing (the level of indemnity should be between a minimum of two months salary for an employee with less than two years seniority up to fourteen months for a seniority above twenty-five years).

[571] These costs would be much higher n case of dismissal of more than three employees within thirty days in company employing fifty employees and over since a social plan will need to be implemented and negotiated with the Workers' Council and the Labour Authorities.

Accounting Methods – Summary of Accounting Principles in France

Background and Development of Accounting Regulations

[572] If accounting obligations for companies are derived in the first instance from legal provisions set out in the French commercial code, the general accounting plan *(Plan Comptable Général, PCG)* is at the heart of the French approach. This plan, originating from a 1999 ruling by the national committee for accounting regulations *(Comité de la réglementation comptable, CRC),* approved by ministerial agreement and published in the official journal *(Journal Officiel),* has been the subject of numerous amendments in order to incorporate new accounting provisions. It is now up to the national accounting standards committee *(Autorité des Normes Comptables, ANC)* to design French accounting regulations applicable to businesses in the private sector. Contrary to situations existing in certain countries where standardisation results from a conceptual framework and a set of standards, the *PCG* provides support for French accounting standards covering the overall accounting process for individual accounts. In so far as consolidated accounts are concerned, a specific regulation *(CRC 99-02)* defines the rules applicable to consolidation which follow the same process as for the PCG in case of amendment.

Presentation of Accounting Regulations

Reporting

[573] All companies are required to draw up their financial statements at least once a year, including a balance sheet, a profit and loss account and official appendix notes in accordance with generally accepted accounting principles in France. Companies using the developed version of the PCG can include a cash flow statement in the appendix notes. Companies listed on the French stock exchange are required to draw up their consolidated accounts in accordance with IFRS standards. Unlisted companies have the option of this method, but only for their consolidated accounts as the presentation of individual accounts in accordance with IFRS standards is not permitted in France.

Accounting Principles

[574] According to Article L. 123-14 of the French commercial code *'the annual accounts must provide a true and fair view of the net worth, financial situation and earnings of the company'.*

[575] In order to guarantee the reliability of the accounting information as described in this text, a certain number of principles must be respected:

- principle of regularity;
- principle of fairness;
- consistency of methods;
- no-netting principle;
- precautionary principle;
- historical cost convention;
- going concern principle;
- booking of costs and profits according to the accruals principle.

Preparation of Consolidated Accounts

[576] Article L.233-16 of the French commercial code requires the preparation and publication of consolidated accounts by companies holding exclusive or joint control of one or several other companies, or over which they have a notable influence.

There are two exceptions however to this rule for unlisted companies:

- company A is itself controlled by company B which includes company A's results in its published consolidated accounts and provided that there is no opposition from shareholders or partners holding at least 10% of share capital;
- the 'group' consisting of company A and its investments does not exceed two out of three of the following criteria over two successive financial years:
  (a) EUR15,000,000 balance sheet total;
  (b) EUR30,000,000 turnover;
  (c) 250 average number of staff.

[577] Other than the cases described in Article L.233-16 of the French commercial code, consolidation of accounts may be carried out on a voluntary basis.

Consolidation Methods

[578] In France, three consolidation methods are possible:

- global integration method in the case of exclusive control;
- proportional integration method in the case of joint control;
- equity method in the case of notable influence.

Accounting of Investments in Consolidated Accounts

Investments: General Principles

- Initial consolidation of a company results from its takeover by the consolidating company.
- Identifiable assets and liabilities are assessed at fair value, that is to say their value in use for investments linked to the general running of the company, and at market value for other investments.

- The residual balance remaining between purchase price of investments and identifiable assets and liabilities corresponds to goodwill, booked in the balance sheet as an asset or as a liability as appropriate.

Investments: 'Pooling of Interests' Method

[579] Regulation *CRC 99-02* paragraph 215 nevertheless provides an optional 'pooling of interests' method to the fair value method when the operation concerned meets certain very strict conditions. In very precise conditions, it has the option of allowing a company's assets and liabilities to be booked at the net book value and not at fair value. This method is applicable under the following conditions:

- purchase is made in one go and must represent at least 90% of capital of the target company;
- remuneration must be made by the immediate or unquestionably deferred issue of shares of a company which is already consolidated and within a maximum time span of five years;
- the balance in cash must not exceed 10% of the total amount of shares issued.

[580] It should be pointed out that this method does not exist under American or IFRS standards.

Mergers and Acquisitions

[581] In France, mergers, acquisitions and business contributions are subject to regulation CRC 04-01 which sets out the accounting method applicable for these types of operations in individual accounts. In so far as the valuation of the contribution for the acquiring company or beneficiary is concerned, it is necessary to analyse the control situation at the time of the operation and to know whether it is a forward operation or backward operation (in the latter case, the shareholder of the business taken over takes control of the acquiring company). For forward and backward operations concerning entities under common control, the contribution must therefore be made at book value. This is also the case for backward operations concerning separately controlled entities. On the other hand, in the case of forward operations concerning separately controlled entities, the contribution must be made at actual value.

[582] In so far as consolidated accounts are concerned and for takeovers carried out via issue of shares (merger, exchange, or partial contribution of assets), it is necessary to refer to the rules set out for the acquisition of shares. It should however be noted that the use of the 'pooling of interests' method is only possible in the case of mergers or equated operations where the valuation of contribution at book value is permitted.

www.ingramcontent.com/pod-product-compliance
Lightning Source LLC
Chambersburg PA
CBHW071350230926
51846CB00002B/501
9789041152695